Referral marketing
Complete Self-Assessment Guide

The guidance in this Self-Assessment is based on Referral marketing best practices and standards in business process architecture, design and quality management. The guidance is also based on the professional judgment of the individual collaborators listed in the Acknowledgments.

Table of Contents

About The Art of Service

The Art of Service, Business Process Architects since 2000, is dedicated to helping stakeholders achieve excellence.

Defining, designing, creating, and implementing a process to solve a stakeholders challenge or meet an objective is the most valuable role... In EVERY group, company, organization and department.

Unless you're talking a one-time, single-use project, there should be a process. Whether that process is managed and implemented by humans, AI, or a combination of the two, it needs to be designed by someone with a complex enough perspective to ask the right questions.

Someone capable of asking the right questions and step back and say, 'What are we really trying to accomplish here? And is there a different way to look at it?'

With The Art of Service's Standard Requirements Self-Assessments, we empower people who can do just that — whether their title is marketer, entrepreneur, manager, salesperson, consultant, Business Process Manager, executive assistant, IT Manager, CIO etc... —they are the people who rule the future. They are people who watch the process as it happens, and ask the right questions to make the process work better.

Contact us when you need any support with this Self-Assessment and any help with templates, blue-prints and examples of standard documents you might need:

http://theartofservice.com
service@theartofservice.com

Acknowledgments

This checklist was developed under the auspices of The Art of Service, chaired by Gerardus Blokdyk.

Representatives from several client companies participated in the preparation of this Self-Assessment.

In addition, we are thankful for the design and printing services provided.

Included Resources - how to access

Included with your purchase of the book is the Referral marketing Self-Assessment Spreadsheet Dashboard which contains all questions and Self-Assessment areas and auto-generates insights, graphs, and project RACI planning - all with examples to get you started right away.

How? Simply send an email to
access@theartofservice.com
with this books' title in the subject to get the Referral marketing Self Assessment Tool right away.

You will receive the following contents with New and Updated specific criteria:

• The latest quick edition of the book in PDF

• The latest complete edition of the book in PDF, which criteria correspond to the criteria in...

• The Self-Assessment Excel Dashboard, and...

• Example pre-filled Self-Assessment Excel Dashboard to get familiar with results generation

• In-depth specific Checklists covering the topic

• Project management checklists and templates to assist with implementation

INCLUDES LIFETIME SELF ASSESSMENT UPDATES

Every self assessment comes with Lifetime Updates and Lifetime Free Updated Books. Lifetime Updates is an industry-first feature which allows you to receive verified self assessment updates, ensuring you always have the most accurate information at your fingertips.

Get it now- you will be glad you did - do it now, before you forget.

Send an email to **access@theartofservice.com** with this books' title in the subject to get the Referral marketing Self Assessment Tool right away.

Your feedback is invaluable to us

If you recently bought this book, we would love to hear from you! You can do this by writing a review on amazon (or the online store where you purchased this book) about your last purchase! As part of our continual service improvement process, we love to hear real client experiences and feedback.

How does it work?
To post a review on Amazon, just log in to your account and click on the Create Your Own Review button (under Customer Reviews) of the relevant product page. You can find examples of product reviews in Amazon. If you purchased from another online store, simply follow their procedures.

What happens when I submit my review?
Once you have submitted your review, send us an email at review@theartofservice.com with the link to your review so we can properly thank you for your feedback.

Purpose of this Self-Assessment

This Self-Assessment has been developed to improve understanding of the requirements and elements of Referral marketing, based on best practices and standards in business process architecture, design and quality management.

It is designed to allow for a rapid Self-Assessment to determine how closely existing management practices and procedures correspond to the elements of the Self-Assessment.

The criteria of requirements and elements of Referral marketing have been rephrased in the format of a Self-Assessment questionnaire, with a seven-criterion scoring system, as explained in this document.

In this format, even with limited background knowledge of

Referral marketing, a manager can quickly review existing operations to determine how they measure up to the standards. This in turn can serve as the starting point of a 'gap analysis' to identify management tools or system elements that might usefully be implemented in the organization to help improve overall performance.

How to use the Self-Assessment

On the following pages are a series of questions to identify to what extent your Referral marketing initiative is complete in comparison to the requirements set in standards.

To facilitate answering the questions, there is a space in front of each question to enter a score on a scale of '1' to '5'.

1 Strongly Disagree

2 Disagree

3 Neutral

4 Agree

5 Strongly Agree

Read the question and rate it with the following in front of mind:

'In my belief,
the answer to this question is clearly defined'.

There are two ways in which you can choose to interpret this statement;
1. how aware are you that the answer to the question is clearly defined
2. for more in-depth analysis you can choose to gather

evidence and confirm the answer to the question. This obviously will take more time, most Self-Assessment users opt for the first way to interpret the question and dig deeper later on based on the outcome of the overall Self-Assessment.

A score of '1' would mean that the answer is not clear at all, where a '5' would mean the answer is crystal clear and defined. Leave emtpy when the question is not applicable or you don't want to answer it, you can skip it without affecting your score. Write your score in the space provided.

After you have responded to all the appropriate statements in each section, compute your average score for that section, using the formula provided, and round to the nearest tenth. Then transfer to the corresponding spoke in the Referral marketing Scorecard on the second next page of the Self-Assessment.

Your completed Referral marketing Scorecard will give you a clear presentation of which Referral marketing areas need attention.

Referral marketing Scorecard Example

Example of how the finalized Scorecard can look like:

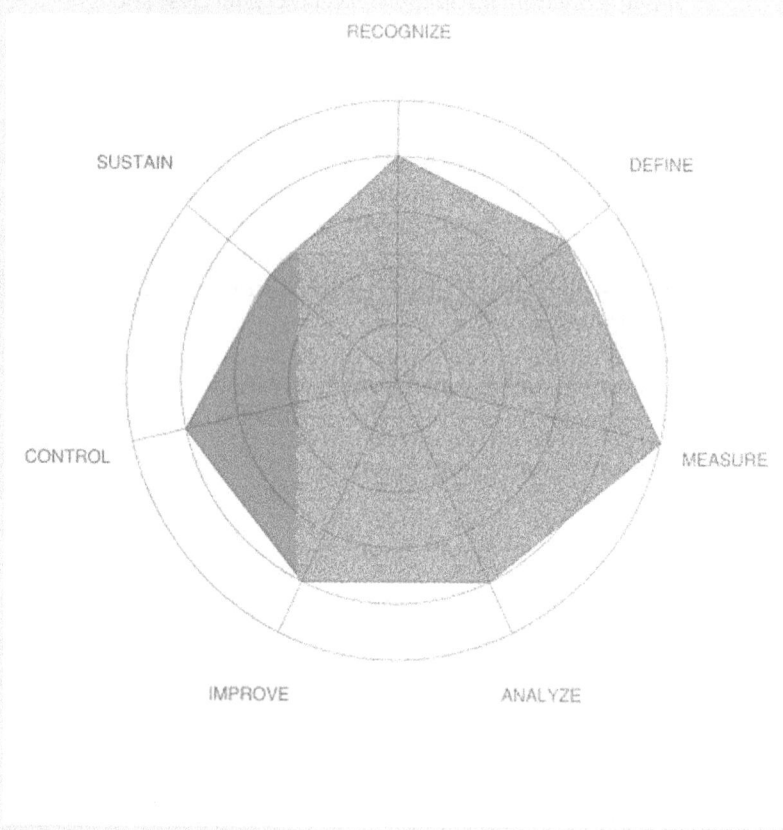

Referral marketing
Scorecard

Your Scores:

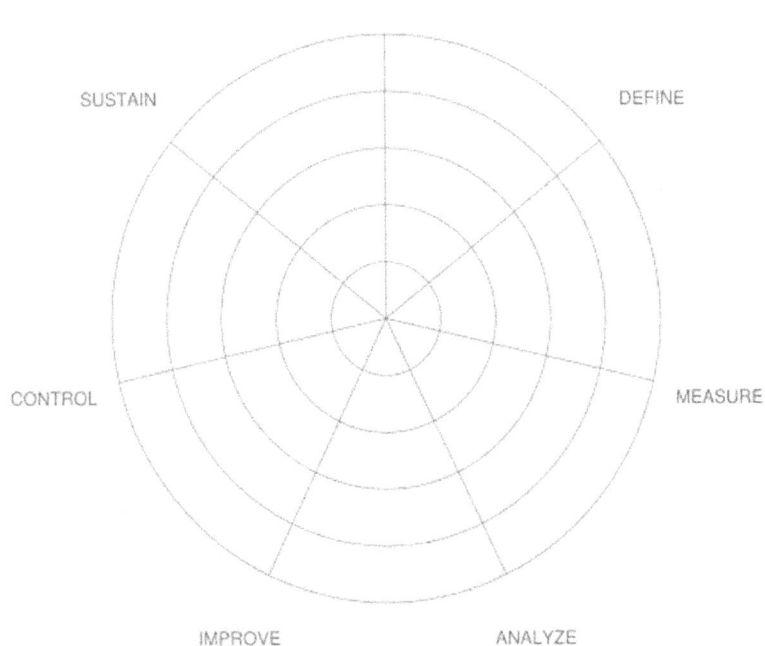

BEGINNING OF THE SELF-ASSESSMENT:

CRITERION #1: RECOGNIZE

INTENT: Be aware of the need for change. Recognize that there is an unfavorable variation, problem or symptom.

In my belief, the answer to this question is clearly defined:

5 Strongly Agree

4 Agree

3 Neutral

2 Disagree

1 Strongly Disagree

1. What do you need to start doing?
<--- Score

2. Will it solve real problems?
<--- Score

3. What are your needs in relation to Referral marketing skills, labor, equipment, and markets?
<--- Score

4. Is the need for organizational change recognized?
<--- Score

5. How are you going to measure success?
<--- Score

6. What are the expected benefits of Referral marketing to the business?
<--- Score

7. Are there Referral marketing problems defined?
<--- Score

8. Do you have/need 24-hour access to key personnel?
<--- Score

9. What are the minority interests and what amount of minority interests can be recognized?
<--- Score

10. When a Referral marketing manager recognizes a problem, what options are available?
<--- Score

11. What vendors make products that address the Referral marketing needs?
<--- Score

12. What information do users need?
<--- Score

13. Who are your key stakeholders who need to sign off?
<--- Score

14. Looking at each person individually – does every one have the qualities which are needed to work in this group?
<--- Score

15. Are controls defined to recognize and contain problems?
<--- Score

16. Who needs to know about Referral marketing?
<--- Score

17. What does Referral marketing success mean to the stakeholders?
<--- Score

18. Can management personnel recognize the monetary benefit of Referral marketing?
<--- Score

19. To what extent does each concerned units management team recognize Referral marketing as an effective investment?
<--- Score

20. Are there any revenue recognition issues?
<--- Score

21. To what extent would your organization benefit from being recognized as a award recipient?
<--- Score

22. Consider your own Referral marketing project, what types of organizational problems do you think might be causing or affecting your problem, based on the work done so far?

<--- Score

23. Will Referral marketing deliverables need to be tested and, if so, by whom?
<--- Score

24. How are the Referral marketing's objectives aligned to the organization's overall business strategy?
<--- Score

25. Should you invest in industry-recognized qualications?
<--- Score

26. What tools and technologies are needed for a custom Referral marketing project?
<--- Score

27. How do you assess your Referral marketing workforce capability and capacity needs, including skills, competencies, and staffing levels?
<--- Score

28. Does Referral marketing create potential expectations in other areas that need to be recognized and considered?
<--- Score

29. Is it clear when you think of the day ahead of you what activities and tasks you need to complete?
<--- Score

30. Does your organization need more Referral marketing education?
<--- Score

31. Will a response program recognize when a crisis occurs and provide some level of response?
<--- Score

32. Are there any specific expectations or concerns about the Referral marketing team, Referral marketing itself?
<--- Score

33. Will new equipment/products be required to facilitate Referral marketing delivery, for example is new software needed?
<--- Score

34. What are the business objectives to be achieved with Referral marketing?
<--- Score

35. Are problem definition and motivation clearly presented?
<--- Score

36. How can auditing be a preventative security measure?
<--- Score

37. What is the smallest subset of the problem you can usefully solve?
<--- Score

38. Are your goals realistic? Do you need to redefine your problem? Perhaps the problem has changed or maybe you have reached your goal and need to set a new one?
<--- Score

39. As a sponsor, customer or management, how important is it to meet goals, objectives?
<--- Score

40. What problems are you facing and how do you consider Referral marketing will circumvent those obstacles?
<--- Score

41. What training and capacity building actions are needed to implement proposed reforms?
<--- Score

42. Who had the original idea?
<--- Score

43. For your Referral marketing project, identify and describe the business environment, is there more than one layer to the business environment?
<--- Score

44. Do you need different information or graphics?
<--- Score

45. Are you dealing with any of the same issues today as yesterday? What can you do about this?
<--- Score

46. Who needs what information?
<--- Score

47. How do you take a forward-looking perspective in identifying Referral marketing research related to market response and models?
<--- Score

48. What do you need to do to get to the point where you can ask?
<--- Score

49. What prevents you from making the changes you know will make you a more effective Referral marketing leader?
<--- Score

50. Are there recognized Referral marketing problems?
<--- Score

51. What else needs to be measured?
<--- Score

52. How does it fit into your organizational needs and tasks?
<--- Score

53. What is the problem or issue?
<--- Score

54. Are employees recognized or rewarded for performance that demonstrates the highest levels of integrity?
<--- Score

55. What extra resources will you need?
<--- Score

56. Who else hopes to benefit from it?
<--- Score

57. What would happen if Referral marketing weren't

done?

<--- Score

58. Who defines the rules in relation to any given issue?

<--- Score

59. How much are sponsors, customers, partners, stakeholders involved in Referral marketing? In other words, what are the risks, if Referral marketing does not deliver successfully?

<--- Score

60. What are the timeframes required to resolve each of the issues/problems?

<--- Score

61. What situation(s) led to this Referral marketing Self Assessment?

<--- Score

62. What should be considered when identifying available resources, constraints, and deadlines?

<--- Score

63. Do you know what you need to know about Referral marketing?

<--- Score

64. Think about the people you identified for your Referral marketing project and the project responsibilities you would assign to them. what kind of training do you think they would need to perform these responsibilities effectively?

<--- Score

65. How do you identify the kinds of information that you will need?
<--- Score

66. What needs to be done?
<--- Score

67. Do you need to avoid or amend any Referral marketing activities?
<--- Score

Add up total points for this section:
_ _ _ _ _ = Total points for this section

Divided by: _ _ _ _ _ _ (number of
statements answered) = _ _ _ _ _ _
Average score for this section

Transfer your score to the Referral
marketing Index at the beginning of the
Self-Assessment.

CRITERION #2: DEFINE:

INTENT: Formulate the business problem. Define the problem, needs and objectives.

In my belief, the answer to this question is clearly defined:

5 Strongly Agree

4 Agree

3 Neutral

2 Disagree

1 Strongly Disagree

1. Is it clearly defined in and to your organization what you do?
<--- Score

2. What is the definition of success?
<--- Score

3. What is the scope?
<--- Score

4. How will the Referral marketing team and the organization measure complete success of Referral marketing?
<--- Score

5. How and when will the baselines be defined?
<--- Score

6. Scope of sensitive information?
<--- Score

7. When are meeting minutes sent out? Who is on the distribution list?
<--- Score

8. Is the team formed and are team leaders (Coaches and Management Leads) assigned?
<--- Score

9. Are required metrics defined, what are they?
<--- Score

10. How often are the team meetings?
<--- Score

11. Are business processes mapped?
<--- Score

12. Has everyone on the team, including the team leaders, been properly trained?
<--- Score

13. How do you gather Referral marketing requirements?
<--- Score

14. When was the Referral marketing start date?
<--- Score

15. How is the team tracking and documenting its work?
<--- Score

16. What system do you use for gathering Referral marketing information?
<--- Score

17. Are accountability and ownership for Referral marketing clearly defined?
<--- Score

18. How was the 'as is' process map developed, reviewed, verified and validated?
<--- Score

19. Is there a critical path to deliver Referral marketing results?
<--- Score

20. How do you hand over Referral marketing context?
<--- Score

21. What constraints exist that might impact the team?
<--- Score

22. Has the improvement team collected the 'voice of the customer' (obtained feedback – qualitative and quantitative)?
<--- Score

23. What was the context?
<--- Score

24. What are the record-keeping requirements of Referral marketing activities?
<--- Score

25. Is data collected and displayed to better understand customer(s) critical needs and requirements.
<--- Score

26. Is the current 'as is' process being followed? If not, what are the discrepancies?
<--- Score

27. Is there regularly 100% attendance at the team meetings? If not, have appointed substitutes attended to preserve cross-functionality and full representation?
<--- Score

28. How does the Referral marketing manager ensure against scope creep?
<--- Score

29. Do the problem and goal statements meet the SMART criteria (specific, measurable, attainable, relevant, and time-bound)?
<--- Score

30. Is there a completed, verified, and validated high-level 'as is' (not 'should be' or 'could be') business process map?
<--- Score

31. In what way can you redefine the criteria of choice clients have in your category in your favor?
<--- Score

32. Is there a Referral marketing management charter, including business case, problem and goal statements, scope, milestones, roles and responsibilities, communication plan?
<--- Score

33. Are improvement team members fully trained on Referral marketing?
<--- Score

34. Will team members perform Referral marketing work when assigned and in a timely fashion?
<--- Score

35. What is the context?
<--- Score

36. Is the team sponsored by a champion or business leader?
<--- Score

37. How will variation in the actual durations of each activity be dealt with to ensure that the expected Referral marketing results are met?
<--- Score

38. What are the compelling business reasons for embarking on Referral marketing?
<--- Score

39. How can the value of Referral marketing be

defined?
<--- Score

40. Have all basic functions of Referral marketing been defined?
<--- Score

41. Does the scope remain the same?
<--- Score

42. Is Referral marketing linked to key business goals and objectives?
<--- Score

43. How would you define the culture at your organization, how susceptible is it to Referral marketing changes?
<--- Score

44. Who defines (or who defined) the rules and roles?
<--- Score

45. How did the Referral marketing manager receive input to the development of a Referral marketing improvement plan and the estimated completion dates/times of each activity?
<--- Score

46. Is there a completed SIPOC representation, describing the Suppliers, Inputs, Process, Outputs, and Customers?
<--- Score

47. What Referral marketing requirements should be gathered?
<--- Score

48. Is the team equipped with available and reliable resources?
<--- Score

49. Is the Referral marketing scope complete and appropriately sized?
<--- Score

50. Is scope creep really all bad news?
<--- Score

51. Are customers identified and high impact areas defined?
<--- Score

52. What critical content must be communicated – who, what, when, where, and how?
<--- Score

53. Is Referral marketing required?
<--- Score

54. What specifically is the problem? Where does it occur? When does it occur? What is its extent?
<--- Score

55. Has a team charter been developed and communicated?
<--- Score

56. What scope to assess?
<--- Score

57. How do you think the partners involved in Referral marketing would have defined success?

<--- Score

58. Are different versions of process maps needed to account for the different types of inputs?
<--- Score

59. Is the scope of Referral marketing defined?
<--- Score

60. What are the rough order estimates on cost savings/opportunities that Referral marketing brings?
<--- Score

61. What are the boundaries of the scope? What is in bounds and what is not? What is the start point? What is the stop point?
<--- Score

62. What sources do you use to gather information for a Referral marketing study?
<--- Score

63. Are there any constraints known that bear on the ability to perform Referral marketing work? How is the team addressing them?
<--- Score

64. Has anyone else (internal or external to the organization) attempted to solve this problem or a similar one before? If so, what knowledge can be leveraged from these previous efforts?
<--- Score

65. What happens if Referral marketing's scope changes?
<--- Score

66. Are team charters developed?
<--- Score

67. Are task requirements clearly defined?
<--- Score

68. What are the tasks and definitions?
<--- Score

69. Is Referral marketing currently on schedule according to the plan?
<--- Score

70. Has the Referral marketing work been fairly and/ or equitably divided and delegated among team members who are qualified and capable to perform the work? Has everyone contributed?
<--- Score

71. Do you all define Referral marketing in the same way?
<--- Score

72. Are resources adequate for the scope?
<--- Score

73. What is out of scope?
<--- Score

74. What is the scope of the Referral marketing effort?
<--- Score

75. Who are the Referral marketing improvement team members, including Management Leads and Coaches?

<--- Score

76. What is in scope?
<--- Score

77. Has/have the customer(s) been identified?
<--- Score

78. Have specific policy objectives been defined?
<--- Score

79. How do you keep key subject matter experts in the loop?
<--- Score

80. Are audit criteria, scope, frequency and methods defined?
<--- Score

81. Has the direction changed at all during the course of Referral marketing? If so, when did it change and why?
<--- Score

82. Is a fully trained team formed, supported, and committed to work on the Referral marketing improvements?
<--- Score

83. What are the dynamics of the communication plan?
<--- Score

84. Have all of the relationships been defined properly?
<--- Score

85. What baselines are required to be defined and managed?
<--- Score

86. What is out-of-scope initially?
<--- Score

87. What are the Roles and Responsibilities for each team member and its leadership? Where is this documented?
<--- Score

88. When is the estimated completion date?
<--- Score

89. Has your scope been defined?
<--- Score

90. Are there different segments of customers?
<--- Score

91. What would be the goal or target for a Referral marketing's improvement team?
<--- Score

92. What defines best in class?
<--- Score

93. If substitutes have been appointed, have they been briefed on the Referral marketing goals and received regular communications as to the progress to date?
<--- Score

94. Who is gathering Referral marketing information?

<--- Score

95. Are customer(s) identified and segmented according to their different needs and requirements?
<--- Score

96. How do you manage scope?
<--- Score

97. Has a high-level 'as is' process map been completed, verified and validated?
<--- Score

98. Has a project plan, Gantt chart, or similar been developed/completed?
<--- Score

99. Will team members regularly document their Referral marketing work?
<--- Score

100. Is full participation by members in regularly held team meetings guaranteed?
<--- Score

101. Are roles and responsibilities formally defined?
<--- Score

102. What key business process output measure(s) does Referral marketing leverage and how?
<--- Score

103. Does the team have regular meetings?
<--- Score

104. Have the customer needs been translated into

specific, measurable requirements? How?
<--- Score

105. What customer feedback methods were used to solicit their input?
<--- Score

106. Is the improvement team aware of the different versions of a process: what they think it is vs. what it actually is vs. what it should be vs. what it could be?
<--- Score

107. What is the scope of Referral marketing?
<--- Score

108. How Much IT Input Is Required to Get a Referral Program up and Running?
<--- Score

109. Why are you doing Referral marketing and what is the scope?
<--- Score

110. Are approval levels defined for contracts and supplements to contracts?
<--- Score

111. Is the Referral marketing scope manageable?
<--- Score

112. What is in the scope and what is not in scope?
<--- Score

113. Is the team adequately staffed with the desired cross-functionality? If not, what additional resources are available to the team?

<--- Score

Add up total points for this section:
_____ = Total points for this section

Divided by: _____ (number of
statements answered) = _____
Average score for this section

Transfer your score to the Referral
marketing Index at the beginning of the
Self-Assessment.

CRITERION #3: MEASURE:

INTENT: Gather the correct data.
Measure the current performance and
evolution of the situation.

In my belief, the answer to this
question is clearly defined:

5 Strongly Agree

4 Agree

3 Neutral

2 Disagree

1 Strongly Disagree

1. What evidence is there and what is measured?
<--- Score

2. Are losses documented, analyzed, and remedial
processes developed to prevent future losses?
<--- Score

3. What are your customers expectations and
measures?

<--- Score

4. What particular quality tools did the team find helpful in establishing measurements?
<--- Score

5. Why do the measurements/indicators matter?
<--- Score

6. Are high impact defects defined and identified in the business process?
<--- Score

7. Which measures and indicators matter?
<--- Score

8. Are there measurements based on task performance?
<--- Score

9. Have all non-recommended alternatives been analyzed in sufficient detail?
<--- Score

10. How do you measure success?
<--- Score

11. Does Referral marketing analysis isolate the fundamental causes of problems?
<--- Score

12. Was a data collection plan established?
<--- Score

13. What are the types and number of measures to use?

<--- Score

14. Did you tackle the cause or the symptom?
<--- Score

15. How do you do risk analysis of rare, cascading, catastrophic events?
<--- Score

16. The approach of traditional Referral marketing works for detail complexity but is focused on a systematic approach rather than an understanding of the nature of systems themselves, what approach will permit your organization to deal with the kind of unpredictable emergent behaviors that dynamic complexity can introduce?
<--- Score

17. What measurements are being captured?
<--- Score

18. How do you identify and analyze stakeholders and their interests?
<--- Score

19. Have you evaluated the costs and benefits associated with outsourcing?
<--- Score

20. Where is it measured?
<--- Score

21. What harm might be caused?
<--- Score

22. What are the key input variables? What are the key

process variables? What are the key output variables?
<--- Score

23. How do you know that any Referral marketing analysis is complete and comprehensive?
<--- Score

24. How frequently do you track Referral marketing measures?
<--- Score

25. Does your organization systematically track and analyze outcomes related for accountability and quality improvement?
<--- Score

26. How do your measurements capture actionable Referral marketing information for use in exceeding your customers expectations and securing your customers engagement?
<--- Score

27. What are the costs of reform?
<--- Score

28. Is data collection planned and executed?
<--- Score

29. Do people already know you and trust you because of your prior business with them?
<--- Score

30. Is there a Performance Baseline?
<--- Score

31. Is it possible to estimate the impact of

unanticipated complexity such as wrong or failed assumptions, feedback, etc. on proposed reforms?
<--- Score

32. Have you found any 'ground fruit' or 'low-hanging fruit' for immediate remedies to the gap in performance?
<--- Score

33. Is key measure data collection planned and executed, process variation displayed and communicated and performance baselined?
<--- Score

34. Is data collected on key measures that were identified?
<--- Score

35. Have you made assumptions about the shape of the future, particularly its impact on your customers and competitors?
<--- Score

36. Are there any easy-to-implement alternatives to Referral marketing? Sometimes other solutions are available that do not require the cost implications of a full-blown project?
<--- Score

37. How will measures be used to manage and adapt?
<--- Score

38. Does Referral marketing systematically track and analyze outcomes for accountability and quality improvement?
<--- Score

39. Does Referral marketing analysis show the relationships among important Referral marketing factors?
<--- Score

40. Do you aggressively reward and promote the people who have the biggest impact on creating excellent Referral marketing services/products?
<--- Score

41. How can you measure Referral marketing in a systematic way?
<--- Score

42. What are the agreed upon definitions of the high impact areas, defect(s), unit(s), and opportunities that will figure into the process capability metrics?
<--- Score

43. Have changes been properly/adequately analyzed for effect?
<--- Score

44. Is a solid data collection plan established that includes measurement systems analysis?
<--- Score

45. What do you measure and why?
<--- Score

46. How large is the gap between current performance and the customer-specified (goal) performance?
<--- Score

47. How do you focus on what is right -not who is right?
<--- Score

48. How do you aggregate measures across priorities?
<--- Score

49. What methods are feasible and acceptable to estimate the impact of reforms?
<--- Score

50. Are missed Referral marketing opportunities costing your organization money?
<--- Score

51. What causes mismanagement?
<--- Score

52. What data was collected (past, present, future/ ongoing)?
<--- Score

53. What causes investor action?
<--- Score

54. Are process variation components displayed/ communicated using suitable charts, graphs, plots?
<--- Score

55. Have the concerns of stakeholders to help identify and define potential barriers been obtained and analyzed?
<--- Score

56. Is long term and short term variability accounted for?

<--- Score

57. How is progress measured?
<--- Score

58. Do staff have the necessary skills to collect, analyze, and report data?
<--- Score

59. Are you taking your company in the direction of better and revenue or cheaper and cost?
<--- Score

60. Are the measurements objective?
<--- Score

61. What are your key Referral marketing organizational performance measures, including key short and longer-term financial measures?
<--- Score

62. Which stakeholder characteristics are analyzed?
<--- Score

63. How to cause the change?
<--- Score

64. How will you measure your Referral marketing effectiveness?
<--- Score

65. What charts has the team used to display the components of variation in the process?
<--- Score

66. How do you stay flexible and focused to recognize

larger Referral marketing results?
<--- Score

67. What could cause delays in the schedule?
<--- Score

68. What disadvantage does this cause for the user?
<--- Score

69. What causes innovation to fail or succeed in your organization?
<--- Score

70. What key measures identified indicate the performance of the business process?
<--- Score

71. How do you measure variability?
<--- Score

72. How will success or failure be measured?
<--- Score

73. How is performance measured?
<--- Score

74. What are the uncertainties surrounding estimates of impact?
<--- Score

75. What is the cost of acquiring a new customer, and the value of each new customer?
<--- Score

76. Can you do Referral marketing without complex (expensive) analysis?

<--- Score

77. What is the right balance of time and resources between investigation, analysis, and discussion and dissemination?
<--- Score

78. Who should receive measurement reports?
<--- Score

79. Who participated in the data collection for measurements?
<--- Score

80. Is the solution cost-effective?
<--- Score

81. How do you control the overall costs of your work processes?
<--- Score

82. What is measured? Why?
<--- Score

83. How is the value delivered by Referral marketing being measured?
<--- Score

84. How do you measure efficient delivery of Referral marketing services?
<--- Score

85. How will your organization measure success?
<--- Score

86. How will you measure success?

<--- Score

87. What would be a real cause for concern?
<--- Score

88. What relevant entities could be measured?
<--- Score

89. How will effects be measured?
<--- Score

90. What are your key Referral marketing indicators that you will measure, analyze and track?
<--- Score

91. Are you aware of what could cause a problem?
<--- Score

92. How can you measure the performance?
<--- Score

93. What is an unallowable cost?
<--- Score

94. Why do you expend time and effort to implement measurement, for whom?
<--- Score

95. What could cause you to change course?
<--- Score

96. What potential environmental factors impact the Referral marketing effort?
<--- Score

97. How are measurements made?

<--- Score

98. What has the team done to assure the stability and accuracy of the measurement process?
<--- Score

99. How do you measure lifecycle phases?
<--- Score

100. What measurements are possible, practicable and meaningful?
<--- Score

101. Does the Referral marketing task fit the client's priorities?
<--- Score

102. Are the units of measure consistent?
<--- Score

103. Have the types of risks that may impact Referral marketing been identified and analyzed?
<--- Score

104. What causes extra work or rework?
<--- Score

105. Do you effectively measure and reward individual and team performance?
<--- Score

106. Are key measures identified and agreed upon?
<--- Score

107. Can you measure the return on analysis?
<--- Score

108. Among the Referral marketing product and service cost to be estimated, which is considered hardest to estimate?
<--- Score

109. Is Process Variation Displayed/Communicated?
<--- Score

Add up total points for this section:
_ _ _ _ _ = Total points for this section

Divided by: _ _ _ _ _ _ (number of statements answered) = _ _ _ _ _ _
Average score for this section

Transfer your score to the Referral marketing Index at the beginning of the Self-Assessment.

CRITERION #4: ANALYZE:

INTENT: Analyze causes, assumptions and hypotheses.

In my belief, the answer to this question is clearly defined:

5 Strongly Agree

4 Agree

3 Neutral

2 Disagree

1 Strongly Disagree

1. Do you, as a leader, bounce back quickly from setbacks?
<--- Score

2. What controls do you have in place to protect data?
<--- Score

3. Do your transactions afford you the ability to capture customer data?
<--- Score

4. What other organizational variables, such as reward systems or communication systems, affect the performance of this Referral marketing process?
<--- Score

5. What behavior drives referrals?
<--- Score

6. What Referral marketing data do you gather or use now?
<--- Score

7. Is the gap/opportunity displayed and communicated in financial terms?
<--- Score

8. What are the revised rough estimates of the financial savings/opportunity for Referral marketing improvements?
<--- Score

9. Referrals play a major role in business development for professional services firms. But what behavior drives such referrals?
<--- Score

10. How do you promote understanding that opportunity for improvement is not criticism of the status quo, or the people who created the status quo?
<--- Score

11. Where is the data coming from to measure compliance?
<--- Score

12. Do your contracts/agreements contain data security obligations?
<--- Score

13. How is the way you as the leader think and process information affecting your organizational culture?
<--- Score

14. What data is gathered?
<--- Score

15. Are gaps between current performance and the goal performance identified?
<--- Score

16. Have any additional benefits been identified that will result from closing all or most of the gaps?
<--- Score

17. What does the data say about the performance of the business process?
<--- Score

18. Was a detailed process map created to amplify critical steps of the 'as is' business process?
<--- Score

19. How do you use Referral marketing data and information to support organizational decision making and innovation?
<--- Score

20. What did the team gain from developing a sub-process map?
<--- Score

21. Is the performance gap determined?

<--- Score

22. Was a cause-and-effect diagram used to explore the different types of causes (or sources of variation)?

<--- Score

23. What is the cost of poor quality as supported by the team's analysis?

<--- Score

24. Do your leaders quickly bounce back from setbacks?

<--- Score

25. How do you identify specific Referral marketing investment opportunities and emerging trends?

<--- Score

26. Have the problem and goal statements been updated to reflect the additional knowledge gained from the analyze phase?

<--- Score

27. An organizationally feasible system request is one that considers the mission, goals and objectives of the organization. Key questions are: is the Referral marketing solution request practical and will it solve a problem or take advantage of an opportunity to achieve company goals?

<--- Score

28. What is your organizations process which leads to recognition of value generation?

<--- Score

29. What conclusions were drawn from the team's data collection and analysis? How did the team reach these conclusions?
<--- Score

30. Is the required Referral marketing data gathered?
<--- Score

31. How was the detailed process map generated, verified, and validated?
<--- Score

32. What were the financial benefits resulting from any 'ground fruit or low-hanging fruit' (quick fixes)?
<--- Score

33. Identify an operational issue in your organization. for example, could a particular task be done more quickly or more efficiently by Referral marketing?
<--- Score

34. How do mission and objectives affect the Referral marketing processes of your organization?
<--- Score

35. Record-keeping requirements flow from the records needed as inputs, outputs, controls and for transformation of a Referral marketing process. Are the records needed as inputs to the Referral marketing process available?
<--- Score

36. Is the Referral marketing process severely broken such that a re-design is necessary?
<--- Score

37. What are your key performance measures or indicators and in-process measures for the control and improvement of your Referral marketing processes?
<--- Score

38. How do you implement and manage your work processes to ensure that they meet design requirements?
<--- Score

39. How often will data be collected for measures?
<--- Score

40. How do your work systems and key work processes relate to and capitalize on your core competencies?
<--- Score

41. What tools were used to generate the list of possible causes?
<--- Score

42. Were there any improvement opportunities identified from the process analysis?
<--- Score

43. Do your employees have the opportunity to do what they do best everyday?
<--- Score

44. What quality tools were used to get through the analyze phase?
<--- Score

45. What will drive Referral marketing change?

<--- Score

46. Are Referral marketing changes recognized early enough to be approved through the regular process?
<--- Score

47. Is the suppliers process defined and controlled?
<--- Score

48. Think about some of the processes you undertake within your organization, which do you own?
<--- Score

49. What process should you select for improvement?
<--- Score

50. What other jobs or tasks affect the performance of the steps in the Referral marketing process?
<--- Score

51. What were the crucial 'moments of truth' on the process map?
<--- Score

52. Did any value-added analysis or 'lean thinking' take place to identify some of the gaps shown on the 'as is' process map?
<--- Score

53. What successful thing are you doing today that may be blinding you to new growth opportunities?
<--- Score

54. What are your Referral marketing processes?
<--- Score

55. Think about the functions involved in your Referral marketing project, what processes flow from these functions?
<--- Score

56. Do several people in different organizational units assist with the Referral marketing process?
<--- Score

57. Were Pareto charts (or similar) used to portray the 'heavy hitters' (or key sources of variation)?
<--- Score

58. What are your current levels and trends in key measures or indicators of Referral marketing product and process performance that are important to and directly serve your customers? How do these results compare with the performance of your competitors and other organizations with similar offerings?
<--- Score

59. What do managers need to do differently to promote positive output WOM?
<--- Score

60. What are the best opportunities for value improvement?
<--- Score

61. Did any additional data need to be collected?
<--- Score

62. Is Data and process analysis, root cause analysis and quantifying the gap/opportunity in place?
<--- Score

63. How is Referral marketing data gathered?
<--- Score

64. Where is Referral marketing data gathered?
<--- Score

65. How do you measure the operational performance of your key work systems and processes, including productivity, cycle time, and other appropriate measures of process effectiveness, efficiency, and innovation?
<--- Score

66. How does the organization define, manage, and improve its Referral marketing processes?
<--- Score

67. What are your best practices for minimizing Referral marketing project risk, while demonstrating incremental value and quick wins throughout the Referral marketing project lifecycle?
<--- Score

68. Can you add value to the current Referral marketing decision-making process (largely qualitative) by incorporating uncertainty modeling (more quantitative)?
<--- Score

69. What methods do you use to gather Referral marketing data?
<--- Score

70. Were any designed experiments used to generate additional insight into the data analysis?
<--- Score

71. How can you accelerate the process?
<--- Score

72. A compounding model resolution with available relevant data can often provide insight towards a solution methodology; which Referral marketing models, tools and techniques are necessary?
<--- Score

73. What tools were used to narrow the list of possible causes?
<--- Score

74. What are your current levels and trends in key Referral marketing measures or indicators of product and process performance that are important to and directly serve your customers?
<--- Score

Add up total points for this section:
_ _ _ _ _ = Total points for this section

Divided by: _ _ _ _ _ _ (number of statements answered) = _ _ _ _ _ _
Average score for this section

Transfer your score to the Referral marketing Index at the beginning of the Self-Assessment.

CRITERION #5: IMPROVE:

INTENT: Develop a practical solution.
Innovate, establish and test the
solution and to measure the results.

In my belief, the answer to this
question is clearly defined:

5 Strongly Agree

4 Agree

3 Neutral

2 Disagree

1 Strongly Disagree

1. What attendant changes will need to be made to
ensure that the solution is successful?
<--- Score

2. Are risk triggers captured?
<--- Score

3. Are you assessing Referral marketing and risk?
<--- Score

4. How will you know that you have improved?
<--- Score

5. How do you improve Referral marketing service perception, and satisfaction?
<--- Score

6. What is the magnitude of the improvements?
<--- Score

7. How did the team generate the list of possible solutions?
<--- Score

8. Are you prepared to handle inbound email responses and questions resulting from your outbound email campaigns?
<--- Score

9. Does the goal represent a desired result that can be measured?
<--- Score

10. Risk Identification: What are the possible risk events your organization faces in relation to Referral marketing?
<--- Score

11. Was a pilot designed for the proposed solution(s)?
<--- Score

12. What were the underlying assumptions on the cost-benefit analysis?
<--- Score

13. Risk factors: what are the characteristics of Referral marketing that make it risky?
<--- Score

14. Is a contingency plan established?
<--- Score

15. Is the scope clearly documented?
<--- Score

16. How do you keep improving Referral marketing?
<--- Score

17. Which of the recognised risks out of all risks can be most likely transferred?
<--- Score

18. What practices helps your organization to develop its capacity to recognize patterns?
<--- Score

19. Who controls the risk?
<--- Score

20. What is the implementation plan?
<--- Score

21. How will the team or the process owner(s) monitor the implementation plan to see that it is working as intended?
<--- Score

22. Risk events: what are the things that could go wrong?
<--- Score

23. Is the implementation plan designed?
<--- Score

24. What sort of results can you expect once you get your referral marketing program?
<--- Score

25. How can you better understand the effects of WOM in influence, recruitment and internal markets?
<--- Score

26. Who are the people involved in developing and implementing Referral marketing?
<--- Score

27. How does the solution remove the key sources of issues discovered in the analyze phase?
<--- Score

28. What actually has to improve and by how much?
<--- Score

29. Is there a cost/benefit analysis of optimal solution(s)?
<--- Score

30. What do you want to improve?
<--- Score

31. To what extent does management recognize Referral marketing as a tool to increase the results?
<--- Score

32. How do you go about comparing Referral marketing approaches/solutions?

<--- Score

33. Are improved process ('should be') maps modified based on pilot data and analysis?
<--- Score

34. How does the team improve its work?
<--- Score

35. How do you Decide on Reward Amounts?
<--- Score

36. How do you measure risk?
<--- Score

37. What resources are required for the improvement efforts?
<--- Score

38. What tools were used to evaluate the potential solutions?
<--- Score

39. What can you do to improve?
<--- Score

40. Is supporting Referral marketing documentation required?
<--- Score

41. What went well, what should change, what can improve?
<--- Score

42. What needs improvement? Why?
<--- Score

43. Who will be responsible for documenting the Referral marketing requirements in detail?
<--- Score

44. Is pilot data collected and analyzed?
<--- Score

45. What tools were used to tap into the creativity and encourage 'outside the box' thinking?
<--- Score

46. What does the 'should be' process map/design look like?
<--- Score

47. If you could go back in time five years, what decision would you make differently? What is your best guess as to what decision you're making today you might regret five years from now?
<--- Score

48. How will you know that a change is an improvement?
<--- Score

49. How will you measure the results?
<--- Score

50. How do you improve your likelihood of success ?
<--- Score

51. How do the Referral marketing results compare with the performance of your competitors and other organizations with similar offerings?
<--- Score

52. How do you improve productivity?
<--- Score

53. What is Referral marketing's impact on utilizing the best solution(s)?
<--- Score

54. Is the optimal solution selected based on testing and analysis?
<--- Score

55. Is there a high likelihood that any recommendations will achieve their intended results?
<--- Score

56. Are new and improved process ('should be') maps developed?
<--- Score

57. How can you improve performance?
<--- Score

58. Will the controls trigger any other risks?
<--- Score

59. Is a solution implementation plan established, including schedule/work breakdown structure, resources, risk management plan, cost/budget, and control plan?
<--- Score

60. What to do with the results or outcomes of measurements?
<--- Score

61. What improvements have been achieved?
<--- Score

62. How do you define the solutions' scope?
<--- Score

63. Why improve in the first place?
<--- Score

64. In the past few months, what is the smallest change you have made that has had the biggest positive result? What was it about that small change that produced the large return?
<--- Score

65. What tools were most useful during the improve phase?
<--- Score

66. How will the organization know that the solution worked?
<--- Score

67. Are there any constraints (technical, political, cultural, or otherwise) that would inhibit certain solutions?
<--- Score

68. What error proofing will be done to address some of the discrepancies observed in the 'as is' process?
<--- Score

69. What lessons, if any, from a pilot were incorporated into the design of the full-scale solution?
<--- Score

70. Explorations of the frontiers of Referral marketing will help you build influence, improve Referral marketing, optimize decision making, and sustain change, what is your approach?
<--- Score

71. For decision problems, how do you develop a decision statement?
<--- Score

72. What are the implications of the one critical Referral marketing decision 10 minutes, 10 months, and 10 years from now?
<--- Score

73. Is the measure of success for Referral marketing understandable to a variety of people?
<--- Score

74. How do you measure progress and evaluate training effectiveness?
<--- Score

75. What is the risk?
<--- Score

76. How do you measure improved Referral marketing service perception, and satisfaction?
<--- Score

77. Is the solution technically practical?
<--- Score

78. What is the Referral marketing's sustainability risk?
<--- Score

79. Is there a small-scale pilot for proposed improvement(s)? What conclusions were drawn from the outcomes of a pilot?
<--- Score

80. Do those selected for the Referral marketing team have a good general understanding of what Referral marketing is all about?
<--- Score

81. What are your current levels and trends in key measures or indicators of workforce and leader development?
<--- Score

82. Who controls key decisions that will be made?
<--- Score

83. How can you improve Referral marketing?
<--- Score

84. Describe the design of the pilot and what tests were conducted, if any?
<--- Score

85. Understanding the Basics of Permission - what is it and why do I need it?
<--- Score

86. What communications are necessary to support the implementation of the solution?
<--- Score

87. What are the results you might expect?
<--- Score

88. Were any criteria developed to assist the team in testing and evaluating potential solutions?
<--- Score

89. Are the best solutions selected?
<--- Score

90. How significant is the improvement in the eyes of the end user?
<--- Score

91. Can the solution be designed and implemented within an acceptable time period?
<--- Score

92. Who will be responsible for making the decisions to include or exclude requested changes once Referral marketing is underway?
<--- Score

93. How can skill-level changes improve Referral marketing?
<--- Score

94. Can you identify any significant risks or exposures to Referral marketing third- parties (vendors, service providers, alliance partners etc) that concern you?
<--- Score

95. What is the team's contingency plan for potential problems occurring in implementation?
<--- Score

96. For estimation problems, how do you develop an estimation statement?
<--- Score

97. How do you decide how much to remunerate an employee?
<--- Score

98. Once you have people in your referral program funnel, what sort of results can you expect in terms of successful referrals and ROI?
<--- Score

99. How do you link measurement and risk?
<--- Score

100. Who will be using the results of the measurement activities?
<--- Score

101. How will you know when its improved?
<--- Score

102. How do you manage and improve your Referral marketing work systems to deliver customer value and achieve organizational success and sustainability?
<--- Score

103. Are possible solutions generated and tested?
<--- Score

Add up total points for this section:
_ _ _ _ _ = Total points for this section

Divided by: _ _ _ _ _ _ (number of statements answered) = _ _ _ _ _ _
Average score for this section

Transfer your score to the Referral

marketing Index at the beginning of the
Self-Assessment.

CRITERION #6: CONTROL:

INTENT: Implement the practical solution. Maintain the performance and correct possible complications.

In my belief, the answer to this question is clearly defined:

5 Strongly Agree

4 Agree

3 Neutral

2 Disagree

1 Strongly Disagree

1. How likely is the current Referral marketing plan to come in on schedule or on budget?
<--- Score

2. How will report readings be checked to effectively monitor performance?
<--- Score

3. In the case of a Referral marketing project, the

criteria for the audit derive from implementation objectives. an audit of a Referral marketing project involves assessing whether the recommendations outlined for implementation have been met. Can you track that any Referral marketing project is implemented as planned, and is it working?
<--- Score

4. Has the improved process and its steps been standardized?
<--- Score

5. What should you measure to verify efficiency gains?
<--- Score

6. Implementation Planning: is a pilot needed to test the changes before a full roll out occurs?
<--- Score

7. Is a response plan established and deployed?
<--- Score

8. What other systems, operations, processes, and infrastructures (hiring practices, staffing, training, incentives/rewards, metrics/dashboards/scorecards, etc.) need updates, additions, changes, or deletions in order to facilitate knowledge transfer and improvements?
<--- Score

9. Does the response plan contain a definite closed loop continual improvement scheme (e.g., plan-do-check-act)?
<--- Score

10. How might the organization capture best practices

and lessons learned so as to leverage improvements across the business?
<--- Score

11. Will your goals reflect your program budget?
<--- Score

12. Will any special training be provided for results interpretation?
<--- Score

13. What is the recommended frequency of auditing?
<--- Score

14. Who controls critical resources?
<--- Score

15. What is the best design framework for Referral marketing organization now that, in a post industrial-age if the top-down, command and control model is no longer relevant?
<--- Score

16. Are documented procedures clear and easy to follow for the operators?
<--- Score

17. What are the critical parameters to watch?
<--- Score

18. Does a troubleshooting guide exist or is it needed?
<--- Score

19. Are you measuring, monitoring and predicting Referral marketing activities to optimize operations and profitability, and enhancing outcomes?

<--- Score

20. Are suggested corrective/restorative actions indicated on the response plan for known causes to problems that might surface?
<--- Score

21. Are there documented procedures?
<--- Score

22. What are you attempting to measure/monitor?
<--- Score

23. How is change control managed?
<--- Score

24. Is there documentation that will support the successful operation of the improvement?
<--- Score

25. Against what alternative is success being measured?
<--- Score

26. Will the team be available to assist members in planning investigations?
<--- Score

27. Are new process steps, standards, and documentation ingrained into normal operations?
<--- Score

28. What quality tools were useful in the control phase?
<--- Score

29. Do you monitor the effectiveness of your Referral marketing activities?
<--- Score

30. Can you adapt and adjust to changing Referral marketing situations?
<--- Score

31. Is there a recommended audit plan for routine surveillance inspections of Referral marketing's gains?
<--- Score

32. Are controls in place and consistently applied?
<--- Score

33. What do you stand for--and what are you against?
<--- Score

34. How many of your stakeholders think that word of mouth just happens, and you don t have any control over it?
<--- Score

35. How do you encourage people to take control and responsibility?
<--- Score

36. Are the planned controls working?
<--- Score

37. How will new or emerging customer needs/requirements be checked/communicated to orient the process toward meeting the new specifications and continually reducing variation?
<--- Score

38. Is there a Referral marketing Communication plan covering who needs to get what information when?
<--- Score

39. Does Referral marketing appropriately measure and monitor risk?
<--- Score

40. Does job training on the documented procedures need to be part of the process team's education and training?
<--- Score

41. Do you Have Control over the Creative and Design Elements of your Referral Program?
<--- Score

42. What is your theory of human motivation, and how does your compensation plan fit with that view?
<--- Score

43. Where do ideas that reach policy makers and planners as proposals for Referral marketing strengthening and reform actually originate?
<--- Score

44. What can you control?
<--- Score

45. Are operating procedures consistent?
<--- Score

46. How will the process owner verify improvement in present and future sigma levels, process capabilities?
<--- Score

47. How do your controls stack up?
<--- Score

48. How will input, process, and output variables be checked to detect for sub-optimal conditions?
<--- Score

49. What can your referral program learn from Google?
<--- Score

50. How will the process owner and team be able to hold the gains?
<--- Score

51. How do you select, collect, align, and integrate Referral marketing data and information for tracking daily operations and overall organizational performance, including progress relative to strategic objectives and action plans?
<--- Score

52. What other areas of the organization might benefit from the Referral marketing team's improvements, knowledge, and learning?
<--- Score

53. What is the control/monitoring plan?
<--- Score

54. Who will be in control?
<--- Score

55. Act/Adjust: What Do you Need to Do Differently?
<--- Score

56. Are the planned controls in place?
<--- Score

57. Does the Referral marketing performance meet the customer's requirements?
<--- Score

58. Have new or revised work instructions resulted?
<--- Score

59. Who is the Referral marketing process owner?
<--- Score

60. Strategic planning in your organization: who are the customers?
<--- Score

61. What adjustments to the strategies are needed?
<--- Score

62. Is there a transfer of ownership and knowledge to process owner and process team tasked with the responsibilities.
<--- Score

63. What should the next improvement project be that is related to Referral marketing?
<--- Score

64. How can you best use all of your knowledge repositories to enhance learning and sharing?
<--- Score

65. Who sets the Referral marketing standards?
<--- Score

66. Do the Referral marketing decisions you make today help people and the planet tomorrow?
<--- Score

67. How do controls support value?
<--- Score

68. How do senior leaders actions reflect a commitment to the organizations Referral marketing values?
<--- Score

69. Is new knowledge gained imbedded in the response plan?
<--- Score

70. What do your reports reflect?
<--- Score

71. Is there a control plan in place for sustaining improvements (short and long-term)?
<--- Score

72. What are the known security controls?
<--- Score

73. Is a response plan in place for when the input, process, or output measures indicate an 'out-of-control' condition?
<--- Score

74. What do you measure to verify effectiveness gains?
<--- Score

75. What key inputs and outputs are being measured

on an ongoing basis?
<--- Score

76. What are the key elements of your Referral marketing performance improvement system, including your evaluation, organizational learning, and innovation processes?
<--- Score

77. Are pertinent alerts monitored, analyzed and distributed to appropriate personnel?
<--- Score

78. Do you monitor the Referral marketing decisions made and fine tune them as they evolve?
<--- Score

79. Is there a documented and implemented monitoring plan?
<--- Score

80. Is knowledge gained on process shared and institutionalized?
<--- Score

81. How do you establish and deploy modified action plans if circumstances require a shift in plans and rapid execution of new plans?
<--- Score

82. How will the day-to-day responsibilities for monitoring and continual improvement be transferred from the improvement team to the process owner?
<--- Score

83. Can support from partners be adjusted?
<--- Score

84. Is there a standardized process?
<--- Score

85. Is reporting being used or needed?
<--- Score

86. How do you monitor?
<--- Score

87. How do you plan on providing proper recognition and disclosure of supporting companies?
<--- Score

88. Who has control over resources?
<--- Score

89. You may have created your quality measures at a time when you lacked resources, technology wasn't up to the required standard, or low service levels were the industry norm. Have those circumstances changed?
<--- Score

90. How will you measure your QA plan's effectiveness?
<--- Score

Add up total points for this section:
_ _ _ _ _ = Total points for this section

Divided by: _ _ _ _ _ _ (number of statements answered) = _ _ _ _ _ _
Average score for this section

Transfer your score to the Referral
marketing Index at the beginning of the
Self-Assessment.

CRITERION #7: SUSTAIN:

INTENT: Retain the benefits.

In my belief, the answer to this question is clearly defined:

5 Strongly Agree

4 Agree

3 Neutral

2 Disagree

1 Strongly Disagree

1. What kind of crime could a potential new hire have committed that would not only not disqualify him/her from being hired by your organization, but would actually indicate that he/she might be a particularly good fit?
<--- Score

2. What goals did you miss?
<--- Score

3. Were lessons learned captured and communicated?

<--- Score

4. What is the best affiliate program to use for a digital download product?
<--- Score

5. Think of your Referral marketing project, what are the main functions?
<--- Score

6. What is an unauthorized commitment?
<--- Score

7. Do you think you know, or do you know you know ?
<--- Score

8. Do you have the right capabilities and capacities?
<--- Score

9. How likely is it that a customer would recommend your company to a friend or colleague?
<--- Score

10. How can you become more high-tech but still be high touch?
<--- Score

11. Did you use your network of contacts to gain business for your company?
<--- Score

12. If you ask your existing customers for referrals, will they think that your business is not doing very well?
<--- Score

13. Why not do Referral marketing?
<--- Score

14. Is Referral marketing realistic, or are you setting yourself up for failure?
<--- Score

15. Who will determine interim and final deadlines?
<--- Score

16. Political -is anyone trying to undermine this project?
<--- Score

17. How do you transition from the baseline to the target?
<--- Score

18. What is your question? Why?
<--- Score

19. What knowledge, skills and characteristics mark a good Referral marketing project manager?
<--- Score

20. Is it economical; do you have the time and money?
<--- Score

21. What are the challenges?
<--- Score

22. When is the best time to ask for referrals?
<--- Score

23. At what moment would you think; Will I get fired?
<--- Score

24. Be aware of what your competitors are doing. When you search for information about your own product or service, which competitors rank highly in the search?
<--- Score

25. Are you / should you be revolutionary or evolutionary?
<--- Score

26. What Are the Biggest Referral Killers?
<--- Score

27. Are you satisfied with your current role? If not, what is missing from it?
<--- Score

28. What is the recommended frequency of auditing?
<--- Score

29. Why is it important to have senior management support for a Referral marketing project?
<--- Score

30. Is word of mouth marketing the number one way that you get customers?
<--- Score

31. Should you promote your referral program to less loyal customers, to reach a broader array of people?
<--- Score

32. Are all key stakeholders present at all Structured Walkthroughs?

<--- Score

33. Do you say no to customers for no reason?
<--- Score

34. Are you making progress, and are you making progress as Referral marketing leaders?
<--- Score

35. How do you cross-sell and up-sell your Referral marketing success?
<--- Score

36. When information truly is ubiquitous, when reach and connectivity are completely global, when computing resources are infinite, and when a whole new set of impossibilities are not only possible, but happening, what will that do to your business?
<--- Score

37. Is there something you wish you would have known when you started trying to get more referrals that you know today?
<--- Score

38. Can you do all this work?
<--- Score

39. How do you deter possible misuse of rewards by referrers?
<--- Score

40. Who have you, as a company, historically been when you've been at your best?
<--- Score

41. What influences the open rate?
<--- Score

42. Are your responses positive or negative?
<--- Score

43. Can you break it down?
<--- Score

44. Are assumptions made in Referral marketing stated explicitly?
<--- Score

45. What may be the consequences for the performance of an organization if all stakeholders are not consulted regarding Referral marketing?
<--- Score

46. Can you maintain your growth without detracting from the factors that have contributed to your success?
<--- Score

47. Why is Referral marketing important for you now?
<--- Score

48. Are you paying enough attention to the partners your company depends on to succeed?
<--- Score

49. Who Should you Promote the Program to?
<--- Score

50. What roles do relationships play in referral marketing?
<--- Score

51. How much time do you devote to your marketing efforts?
<--- Score

52. Would you rather sell to knowledgeable and informed customers or to uninformed customers?
<--- Score

53. What is something you believe that nearly no one agrees with you on?
<--- Score

54. How do you make it meaningful in connecting Referral marketing with what users do day-to-day?
<--- Score

55. How are you doing compared to your industry?
<--- Score

56. What happens if you do not have enough funding?
<--- Score

57. What are the business goals Referral marketing is aiming to achieve?
<--- Score

58. What are the antecedents of WOM?
<--- Score

59. How do you sketch out a successful rewards program?
<--- Score

60. What are the must haves for your successful

referral marketing strategy?

<--- Score

61. Should you Really Be Rewarding Referral Behavior?

<--- Score

62. Will it be accepted by users?

<--- Score

63. What have you done to protect your business from competitive encroachment?

<--- Score

64. How High is your un-subscribe/opt-out rate?

<--- Score

65. What aspect of your reputation is most important?

<--- Score

66. What are the success criteria that will indicate that Referral marketing objectives have been met and the benefits delivered?

<--- Score

67. Are the rewards for this referral program on brand?

<--- Score

68. What would a good guarantee be?

<--- Score

69. If word of mouth marketing is not how you get customers, what marketing do you do?

<--- Score

70. What do we do when new problems arise?
<--- Score

71. Who are your customers?
<--- Score

72. What will be the consequences to the stakeholder (financial, reputation etc) if Referral marketing does not go ahead or fails to deliver the objectives?
<--- Score

73. Who do we want your customers to become?
<--- Score

74. What are the long-term Referral marketing goals?
<--- Score

75. Which functions and people interact with the supplier and or customer?
<--- Score

76. What is the kind of project structure that would be appropriate for your Referral marketing project, should it be formal and complex, or can it be less formal and relatively simple?
<--- Score

77. Why will customers want to buy your organizations products/services?
<--- Score

78. Is your physical address included in your email campaign?
<--- Score

79. How will you motivate the stakeholders with the least vested interest?
<--- Score

80. Which Referral marketing goals are the most important?
<--- Score

81. Operational - will it work?
<--- Score

82. If you weren't already in this business, would you enter it today? And if not, what are you going to do about it?
<--- Score

83. Ultimately how does incentive influence the referral behavior?
<--- Score

84. How can you become the company that would put you out of business?
<--- Score

85. Are you changing as fast as the world around you?
<--- Score

86. Who else should you help?
<--- Score

87. If you were responsible for initiating and implementing major changes in your organization, what steps might you take to ensure acceptance of those changes?
<--- Score

88. Do Referral marketing rules make a reasonable demand on a users capabilities?
<--- Score

89. Why should people listen to you?
<--- Score

90. If you got fired and a new hire took your place, what would she do different?
<--- Score

91. When starting your business, where did your first clients come from?
<--- Score

92. What happens when a new employee joins the organization?
<--- Score

93. Is referral marketing right for your business?
<--- Score

94. What you are going to do to affect the numbers?
<--- Score

95. How will you ensure you get what you expected?
<--- Score

96. What current systems have to be understood and/or changed?
<--- Score

97. Who is responsible for ensuring appropriate resources (time, people and money) are allocated to Referral marketing?
<--- Score

98. What is the craziest thing you can do?
<--- Score

99. Is a Referral marketing team work effort in place?
<--- Score

100. What threat is Referral marketing addressing?
<--- Score

101. Does WOM co-vary mored irectly with perception,or disconfirmation, or value, satisfaction,or quality?
<--- Score

102. How can you incorporate support to ensure safe and effective use of Referral marketing into the services that you provide?
<--- Score

103. What information is critical to your organization that your executives are ignoring?
<--- Score

104. Is your annual transaction size large enough and/or frequent enough to warrant rewards?
<--- Score

105. Instead of going to current contacts for new ideas, what if you reconnected with dormant contacts--the people you used to know? If you were going reactivate a dormant tie, who would it be?
<--- Score

106. What are the potential basics of Referral marketing fraud?

<--- Score

107. What is the funding source for this project?
<--- Score

108. Once your program is up and running what do you do?
<--- Score

109. When is your audience most likely to read what you are sending them?
<--- Score

110. Is there any reason to believe the opposite of my current belief?
<--- Score

111. If you are not sure which sources to try, look for your ideal prospect. Where do they hang out online and off?
<--- Score

112. What are the benefits of adopting students as brand advocates?
<--- Score

113. What counts that you are not counting?
<--- Score

114. How do you know if you are successful?
<--- Score

115. Can the schedule be done in the given time?
<--- Score

116. How does Referral marketing integrate with

other business initiatives?

<--- Score

117. What trouble can you get into?

<--- Score

118. Which individuals, teams or departments will be involved in Referral marketing?

<--- Score

119. Will you have to monopolize your IT team for a few weeks to establish the program?

<--- Score

120. If you had to leave your organization for a year and the only communication you could have with employees/colleagues was a single paragraph, what would you write?

<--- Score

121. How does WOM operate in cultures other than Western?

<--- Score

122. How do you deliver?

<--- Score

123. What is the source of the strategies for Referral marketing strengthening and reform?

<--- Score

124. How do you foster the skills, knowledge, talents, attributes, and characteristics you want to have?

<--- Score

125. What are strategies for increasing support and

reducing opposition?
<--- Score

126. What are you challenging?
<--- Score

127. What kills your chances of getting referrals?
<--- Score

128. How do you assess the Referral marketing pitfalls that are inherent in implementing it?
<--- Score

129. Who is responsible for errors?
<--- Score

130. Have you assigned a single person to champion, oversee, and be responsible for referral marketing?
<--- Score

131. What are the short and long-term Referral marketing goals?
<--- Score

132. Ask yourself: how would you do this work if you only had one staff member to do it?
<--- Score

133. Are you asking; Thank you for your business, how can I help you or Is there some way I can help you grow your business?
<--- Score

134. In retrospect, of the projects that you pulled the plug on, what percent do you wish had been allowed

to keep going, and what percent do you wish had ended earlier?

<--- Score

135. How valuable are loyal customers?

<--- Score

136. How much contingency will be available in the budget?

<--- Score

137. What percent of your referrals become paying customers or clients?

<--- Score

138. If your company went out of business tomorrow, would anyone who doesn't get a paycheck here care?

<--- Score

139. What is it like to work for you?

<--- Score

140. What projects are going on in the organization today, and what resources are those projects using from the resource pools?

<--- Score

141. Are you prepared to handle all unsubscribe requests within 10 days of the request?

<--- Score

142. Who is the main stakeholder, with ultimate responsibility for driving Referral marketing forward?

<--- Score

143. What trophy do you want on your mantle?

<--- Score

144. How many referrals have you received in the last six months?

<--- Score

145. Do you have past Referral marketing successes?

<--- Score

146. How is intention to increase WOM connected to actual performance?

<--- Score

147. Where do you feel successful in your business?

<--- Score

148. What are the key enablers to make this Referral marketing move?

<--- Score

149. How do you set Referral marketing stretch targets and how do you get people to not only participate in setting these stretch targets but also that they strive to achieve these?

<--- Score

150. What are the barriers to increased Referral marketing production?

<--- Score

151. Will digital advertising be a medium used with the various populations?

<--- Score

152. What would you recommend your friend do if he/

she were facing this dilemma?
<--- Score

153. What is a feasible sequencing of reform initiatives over time?
<--- Score

154. How comfortable are you about asking your clients for referrals?
<--- Score

155. How will you know that the Referral marketing project has been successful?
<--- Score

156. Are there any activities that you can take off your to do list?
<--- Score

157. What relationships among Referral marketing trends do you perceive?
<--- Score

158. Where can you break convention?
<--- Score

159. What Referral marketing modifications can you make work for you?
<--- Score

160. How do you lead with Referral marketing in mind?
<--- Score

161. Business offers us constant contact with other people, but how often do you have a chance to

show some compassion during that contact?
<--- Score

162. How do you provide a safe environment
-physically and emotionally?
<--- Score

163. Whose voice (department, ethnic group, women, older workers, etc) might you have missed hearing from in your company, and how might you amplify this voice to create positive momentum for your business?
<--- Score

164. How much are you paying, on average, for each customer acquisition?
<--- Score

165. Is the impact that Referral marketing has shown?
<--- Score

166. Have new benefits been realized?
<--- Score

167. What happens at your organization when people fail?
<--- Score

168. How effective are existing referral programmes in generating enquiries,trial, retention and switching behaviours?
<--- Score

169. What stupid rule would you most like to kill?
<--- Score

170. What are the gaps in your knowledge and experience?
<--- Score

171. What should you stop doing?
<--- Score

172. Whom among your colleagues do you trust, and for what?
<--- Score

173. Do you integrate social media with your traditional marketing programs?
<--- Score

174. Who do you think the world wants your organization to be?
<--- Score

175. What must you excel at?
<--- Score

176. What did you miss in the interview for the worst hire you ever made?
<--- Score

177. What are the rules and assumptions your industry operates under? What if the opposite were true?
<--- Score

178. How Much Effort Is It to Maintain your Referral Program?
<--- Score

179. How do you currently use word of mouth or referral marketing tactics?

<--- Score

180. How do you keep the momentum going?
<--- Score

181. How long will it take to change?
<--- Score

182. Have you previewed and sent yourself a test mailing?
<--- Score

183. Start with your customers. Who are they, what are they likely to be looking for online and how do they like to purchase?
<--- Score

184. How do you proactively clarify deliverables and Referral marketing quality expectations?
<--- Score

185. What are your goals?
<--- Score

186. What is the range of capabilities?
<--- Score

187. How do you govern and fulfill your societal responsibilities?
<--- Score

188. What are the usability implications of Referral marketing actions?
<--- Score

189. Do you know what you are doing? And who do

you call if you don't?
<--- Score

190. If no one would ever find out about your accomplishments, how would you lead differently?
<--- Score

191. What kills your chance of getting referrals?
<--- Score

192. Where do prospects hang out online and offline?
<--- Score

193. What Referral marketing skills are most important?
<--- Score

194. Its obvious that you should reward the referrer. But should you also reward the new prospect?
<--- Score

195. Do you think Referral marketing accomplishes the goals you expect it to accomplish?
<--- Score

196. Have benefits been optimized with all key stakeholders?
<--- Score

197. Who are your current customers?
<--- Score

198. Are new benefits received and understood?
<--- Score

199. Are others happy with your work?
<--- Score

200. What is the attitude of the referring customer and the referred customer to your programmes and to the stakeholders sponsoring the programmes?
<--- Score

201. How can you negotiate Referral marketing successfully with a stubborn boss, an irate client, or a deceitful coworker?
<--- Score

202. Are you maintaining a past–present–future perspective throughout the Referral marketing discussion?
<--- Score

203. If your customer were your grandmother, would you tell her to buy what you're selling?
<--- Score

204. Is the Referral marketing organization completing tasks effectively and efficiently?
<--- Score

205. Do you use personalized links (PURLs) as part of its promotional effort?
<--- Score

206. Are the assumptions believable and achievable?
<--- Score

207. Do you feel that more should be done in the

Referral marketing area?
<--- Score

208. Are you offering something to the current customer as well as to the new customer that is getting referred?
<--- Score

209. Do you see more potential in people than they do in themselves?
<--- Score

210. What unique value proposition (UVP) do you offer?
<--- Score

211. How do you determine the key elements that affect Referral marketing workforce satisfaction, how are these elements determined for different workforce groups and segments?
<--- Score

212. What are specific Referral marketing rules to follow?
<--- Score

213. Which antecedent marketing conditions are most closely associated with WOM?
<--- Score

214. What is Your Story?
<--- Score

215. If there were zero limitations, what would you do differently?
<--- Score

216. What new services of functionality will be implemented next with Referral marketing ?
<--- Score

217. Does Reciprocity Affect Referral Generation?
<--- Score

218. What pitfalls have you faced with trying to get more referrals?
<--- Score

219. Where do you spend money on marketing today?
<--- Score

220. What one word do you want to own in the minds of your customers, employees, and partners?
<--- Score

221. What is the timeline for referral marketing?
<--- Score

222. How fresh are your email addresses?
<--- Score

223. Have you used appropriate graphics while also making good use of white space?
<--- Score

224. How do you accomplish your long range Referral marketing goals?
<--- Score

225. Do you use a multi-functional perspective in organizing referral marketing?

<--- Score

226. Where do you go for regular up to date advice?
<--- Score

227. What have been your experiences in defining long range Referral marketing goals?
<--- Score

228. Who is on the team?
<--- Score

229. What management system can you use to leverage the Referral marketing experience, ideas, and concerns of the people closest to the work to be done?
<--- Score

230. What business benefits will Referral marketing goals deliver if achieved?
<--- Score

231. Are you using a design thinking approach and integrating Innovation, Referral marketing Experience, and Brand Value?
<--- Score

232. What is your formula for success in Referral marketing ?
<--- Score

233. How do you listen to customers to obtain actionable information?
<--- Score

234. Why should you adopt a Referral marketing framework?
<--- Score

235. How effective are existing referral programmes in generating enquiries, trial, retention and switching behaviours?
<--- Score

236. How do you deal with Referral marketing changes?
<--- Score

237. How do you engage the workforce, in addition to satisfying them?
<--- Score

238. How will you insure seamless interoperability of Referral marketing moving forward?
<--- Score

239. What are the antecedents of WOM; and, what are the consequences of WOM?
<--- Score

240. Did your employees make progress today?
<--- Score

241. What are you trying to prove to yourself, and how might it be hijacking your life and business success?
<--- Score

242. How do you get influencers to recommend your organization?
<--- Score

243. Why referrals instead of advertising?
<--- Score

244. How do you ensure that implementations of Referral marketing products are done in a way that ensures safety?
<--- Score

245. What are internal and external Referral marketing relations?
<--- Score

246. Where Are Your Prospects?
<--- Score

247. What is your BATNA (best alternative to a negotiated agreement)?
<--- Score

248. How do customers see your organization?
<--- Score

249. How do you stay inspired?
<--- Score

250. What Role Does Reputation Play?
<--- Score

251. How valuable is word of mouth?
<--- Score

252. What are the essentials of internal Referral marketing management?
<--- Score

253. Which models, tools and techniques are

necessary?
<--- Score

254. Has implementation been effective in reaching specified objectives so far?
<--- Score

255. How do you track customer value, profitability or financial return, organizational success, and sustainability?
<--- Score

256. What Role Do Relationships Play?
<--- Score

257. Are you relevant? Will you be relevant five years from now? Ten?
<--- Score

258. Who, on the executive team or the board, has spoken to a customer recently?
<--- Score

259. How will you build an effective referral program that actually works?
<--- Score

260. Is your Subject line straightforward, vs. misleading?
<--- Score

261. Who are your most important consumers?
<--- Score

262. What was the last experiment you ran?
<--- Score

263. How is implementation research currently incorporated into each of your goals?
<--- Score

264. Is Referral marketing dependent on the successful delivery of a current project?
<--- Score

265. To whom do you add value?
<--- Score

266. How do you Integrate several referral programs?
<--- Score

267. If you do not follow, then how to lead?
<--- Score

268. Do you have enough freaky customers in your portfolio pushing you to the limit day in and day out?
<--- Score

269. How do you create buy-in?
<--- Score

270. What do prospects want or what would help them in a significant way?
<--- Score

271. Is maximizing Referral marketing protection the same as minimizing Referral marketing loss?
<--- Score

272. What is the purpose of Referral marketing in relation to the mission?

<--- Score

273. In the past year, what have you done (or could you have done) to increase the accurate perception of your company/brand as ethical and honest?
<--- Score

274. Who will manage the integration of tools?
<--- Score

275. What are current Referral marketing paradigms?
<--- Score

276. What are your most important goals for the strategic Referral marketing objectives?
<--- Score

277. In a project to restructure Referral marketing outcomes, which stakeholders would you involve?
<--- Score

278. What role does communication play in the success or failure of a Referral marketing project?
<--- Score

279. Have you used valid From and Reply addresses?
<--- Score

280. Have you checked all links to be sure they work properly?
<--- Score

281. Do you have the right people on the bus?
<--- Score

282. Who will be responsible for deciding whether Referral marketing goes ahead or not after the initial investigations?
<--- Score

283. How do you go about securing Referral marketing?
<--- Score

284. What would have to be true for the option on the table to be the best possible choice?
<--- Score

285. Is your basic point _____ or _____?
<--- Score

286. Does your email include a way for recipients to unsubscribe?
<--- Score

287. Is there a work around that you can use?
<--- Score

288. Who are four people whose careers you have enhanced?
<--- Score

289. How important is Referral marketing to the user organizations mission?
<--- Score

290. What potential megatrends could make your business model obsolete?
<--- Score

291. Who uses your product in ways you never

expected?
<--- Score

292. What does your signature ensure?
<--- Score

293. What is your competitive advantage?
<--- Score

294. Who is responsible for Referral marketing?
<--- Score

295. Which is better at predicting intention to utter WOM or actual behaviour: the disconfirmation or attitudinal paradigm?
<--- Score

296. How much does Referral marketing help?
<--- Score

297. Do you have an online digital presence that allows you to interact with your customers?
<--- Score

298. Who are the key stakeholders?
<--- Score

299. What is the budget?
<--- Score

300. Marketing budgets are tighter, consumers are more skeptical, and social media has changed forever the way we talk about Referral marketing. How do you gain traction?
<--- Score

301. Will there be any necessary staff changes (redundancies or new hires)?
<--- Score

302. Who will provide the final approval of Referral marketing deliverables?
<--- Score

303. Do you have an implicit bias for capital investments over people investments?
<--- Score

304. What is effective Referral marketing?
<--- Score

305. Are there any disadvantages to implementing Referral marketing? There might be some that are less obvious?
<--- Score

306. Are the criteria for selecting recommendations stated?
<--- Score

307. How do you maintain Referral marketing's Integrity?
<--- Score

308. What are the top 3 things at the forefront of your Referral marketing agendas for the next 3 years?
<--- Score

309. Who do you want your customers to become?
<--- Score

310. The best motivating offer is one that truly

helps out the referrer. What do others want or what would help them in a significant way?
<--- Score

311. When you map the key players in your own work and the types/domains of relationships with them, which relationships do you find easy and which challenging, and why?
<--- Score

312. What is the most common challenge?
<--- Score

313. What is the estimated value of the project?
<--- Score

314. How do you foster innovation?
<--- Score

315. What are your personal philosophies regarding Referral marketing and how do they influence your work?
<--- Score

316. How do you keep records, of what?
<--- Score

317. Why do and why don't your customers like your organization?
<--- Score

Add up total points for this section:
_ _ _ _ _ = Total points for this section

Divided by: _ _ _ _ _ _ (number of statements answered) = _ _ _ _ _ _

Average score for this section

**Transfer your score to the Referral
marketing Index at the beginning of the
Self-Assessment.**

Referral marketing and Managing Projects, Criteria for Project Managers:

1.0 Initiating Process Group: Referral marketing

1. How well did you do?

2. If the risk event occurs, what will you do?

3. In which Referral marketing project management process group is the detailed Referral marketing project budget created?

4. Are you properly tracking the progress of the Referral marketing project and communicating the status to stakeholders?

5. What are the pressing issues of the hour?

6. When will the Referral marketing project be done?

7. Will the Referral marketing project meet the client requirements, and will it achieve the business success criteria that justified doing the Referral marketing project in the first place?

8. Where must it be done?

9. Mitigate. what will you do to minimize the impact should the risk event occur?

10. During which stage of Risk planning are risks prioritized based on probability and impact?

11. Who is funding the Referral marketing project?

12. What were things that you need to improve?

13. Are identified risks being monitored properly, are new risks arising during the Referral marketing project or are foreseen risks occurring?

14. Who is behind the Referral marketing project?

15. Do you know the roles & responsibilities required for this Referral marketing project?

16. Were sponsors and decision makers available when needed outside regularly scheduled meetings?

17. How do you help others satisfy needs?

18. What do they need to know about the Referral marketing project?

19. Were escalated issues resolved promptly?

20. Do you know all the stakeholders impacted by the Referral marketing project and what needs are?

1.1 Project Charter: Referral marketing

21. Must Have?

22. Why executive support?

23. Why have you chosen the aim you have set forth?

24. What is the most common tool for helping define the detail?

25. Customer: who are you doing the Referral marketing project for?

26. Does the Referral marketing project need to consider any special capacity or capability issues?

27. What are the known stakeholder requirements?

28. When is a charter needed?

29. How much?

30. Who will take notes, document decisions?

31. Why is it important?

32. Is time of the essence?

33. Major high-level milestone targets: what events measure progress?

34. Who manages integration?

35. What material?

36. What are the deliverables?

37. Referral marketing project deliverables: what is the Referral marketing project going to produce?

38. Why Outsource?

39. Who are the stakeholders?

40. How will you know that a change is an improvement?

1.2 Stakeholder Register: Referral marketing

41. How should employers make voices heard?

42. How much influence do they have on the Referral marketing project?

43. What are the major Referral marketing project milestones requiring communications or providing communications opportunities?

44. Who wants to talk about Security?

45. How big is the gap?

46. What is the power of the stakeholder?

47. How will reports be created?

48. What opportunities exist to provide communications?

49. What & Why?

50. Who is managing stakeholder engagement?

51. Is your organization ready for change?

1.3 Stakeholder Analysis Matrix: Referral marketing

52. Market developments?

53. Lack of competitive strength?

54. Arena: in what fields are the actors active, where are they present?

55. How do customers express needs?

56. What should thwe organizations stakeholders avoid?

57. Beneficiaries; who are the potential beneficiaries?

58. Which conditions out of the control of the management are crucial for the sustainability of its effects?

59. What makes a person a stakeholder?

60. Participatory approach: how will key stakeholders participate in the Referral marketing project?

61. Who holds positions of responsibility in interested organizations?

62. What do people from other organizations see as your strengths?

63. What is your Advocacy Strategy?

64. Information and research?

65. What is the stakeholders power and status in relation to the Referral marketing project?

66. Market demand?

67. How are the threatened Referral marketing project targets being used?

68. Who will obstruct/hinder the Referral marketing project if they are not involved?

69. What is relationship with the Referral marketing project?

70. Why do you need to manage Referral marketing project Risk?

71. How will the stakeholder directly benefit from the Referral marketing project and how will this affect the stakeholders motivation?

2.0 Planning Process Group: Referral marketing

72. To what extent have public/private national resources and/or counterparts been mobilized to contribute to the programs objective and produce results and impacts?

73. Are work methodologies, financial instruments, etc. shared among departments, organizations and Referral marketing projects?

74. How well will the chosen processes produce the expected results?

75. What will you do?

76. Are there efficient coordination mechanisms to avoid overloading the counterparts, participating stakeholders?

77. Is the pace of implementing the products of the program ensuring the completeness of the results of the Referral marketing project?

78. What do they need to know about the Referral marketing project?

79. Are you just doing busywork to pass the time?

80. Professionals want to know what is expected from them; what are the deliverables?

81. When developing the estimates for Referral marketing project phases, you choose to add the individual estimates for the activities that comprise each phase. What type of estimation method are you using?

82. To what extent and in what ways are the Referral marketing project contributing to progress towards organizational reform?

83. Who are the Referral marketing project stakeholders?

84. How will you know you did it?

85. Explanation: is what the Referral marketing project intents to solve a hard question?

86. What is the NEXT thing to do?

87. What will you do to minimize the impact should a risk event occur?

88. Why is it important to determine activity sequencing on Referral marketing projects?

89. In what ways can the governance of the Referral marketing project be improved so that it has greater likelihood of achieving future sustainability?

90. When will the Referral marketing project be done?

91. What is the difference between the early schedule and late schedule?

2.1 Project Management Plan: Referral marketing

92. What did not work so well?

93. Do there need to be organizational changes?

94. How well are you able to manage your risk?

95. What does management expect of PMs?

96. Are cost risk analysis methods applied to develop contingencies for the estimated total Referral marketing project costs?

97. When is the Referral marketing project management plan created?

98. What happened during the process that you found interesting?

99. Where does all this information come from?

100. What data/reports/tools/etc. do your PMs need?

101. If the Referral marketing project management plan is a comprehensive document that guides you in Referral marketing project execution and control, then what should it NOT contain?

102. How can you best help your organization to develop consistent practices in Referral marketing project management planning stages?

103. Are alternatives safe, functional, constructible, economical, reasonable and sustainable?

104. What went wrong?

105. Are there non-structural buyout or relocation recommendations?

106. Is mitigation authorized or recommended?

107. What goes into your Referral marketing project Charter?

108. What is the business need?

109. Are there any windfall benefits that would accrue to the Referral marketing project sponsor or other parties?

2.2 Scope Management Plan: Referral marketing

110. Are enough systems & user personnel assigned to the Referral marketing project?

111. Timeline and milestones?

112. Are there any scope changes proposed for the previously authorized Referral marketing project?

113. Is quality monitored from the perspective of the customers needs and expectations?

114. What are the risks that could significantly affect the scope of the Referral marketing project?

115. Describe the process for accepting the Referral marketing project deliverables. Will the Referral marketing project deliverables become accepted in writing?

116. Staffing Requirements?

117. Are issues raised, assessed, actioned, and resolved in a timely and efficient manner?

118. Does the title convey to the reader the essence of the Referral marketing project?

119. Have external dependencies been captured in the schedule?

120. What is your organizations history in doing similar activities?

121. Are changes in scope (deliverable commitments) agreed to by all affected groups & individuals?

122. Personnel with expertise?

123. Materials available for performing the work?

124. Alignment to strategic goals & objectives?

125. Has stakeholder analysis been conducted, assessing influence on the Referral marketing project and authority levels?

126. Knowing the health of the Referral marketing project – What is the status?

127. Is pert / critical path or equivalent methodology being used?

128. Have key stakeholders been identified?

129. Has process improvement efforts been completed before requirements efforts begin?

2.3 Requirements Management Plan: Referral marketing

130. Did you provide clear and concise specifications?

131. After the requirements are gathered and set forth on the requirements register, theyre little more than a laundry list of items. Some may be duplicates, some might conflict with others and some will be too broad or too vague to understand. Describe how the requirements will be analyzed. Who will perform the analysis?

132. Is the system software (non-operating system) new to the IT Referral marketing project team?

133. Who is responsible for quantifying the Referral marketing project requirements?

134. Who will finally present the work or product(s) for acceptance?

135. Do you really need to write this document at all?

136. How will you develop the schedule of requirements activities?

137. Who is responsible for monitoring and tracking the Referral marketing project requirements?

138. Who has the authority to reject Referral marketing project requirements?

139. How do you know that you have done this right?

140. Could inaccurate or incomplete requirements in this Referral marketing project create a serious risk for the business?

141. Are all the stakeholders ready for the transition into the user community?

142. Do you have price sheets and a methodology for determining the total proposal cost?

143. Is it new or replacing an existing business system or process?

144. Will the contractors involved take full responsibility?

145. What cost metrics will be used?

146. Is the change control process documented?

147. How will you communicate scheduled tasks to other team members?

148. Controlling Referral marketing project requirements involves monitoring the status of the Referral marketing project requirements and managing changes to the requirements. Who is responsible for monitoring and tracking the Referral marketing project requirements?

149. Is there formal agreement on who has authority to approve a change in requirements?

2.4 Requirements Documentation: Referral marketing

150. Where are business rules being captured?

151. Is your business case still valid?

152. What if the system wasn t implemented?

153. Does the system provide the functions which best support the customers needs?

154. Consistency. are there any requirements conflicts?

155. How does what is being described meet the business need?

156. Who is interacting with the system?

157. Can the requirements be checked?

158. How will requirements be documented and who signs off on them?

159. What will be the integration problems?

160. How linear / iterative is your Requirements Gathering process (or will it be)?

161. Where do system and software requirements come from, what are sources?

162. Is new technology needed?

163. How to document system requirements?

164. What marketing channels do you want to use: e-mail, letter or sms?

165. Have the benefits identified with the system being identified clearly?

166. Is the origin of the requirement clearly stated?

167. Are there any requirements conflicts?

168. Is the requirement realistically testable?

169. Completeness. are all functions required by the customer included?

2.5 Requirements Traceability Matrix: Referral marketing

170. Do you have a clear understanding of all subcontracts in place?

171. Will you use a Requirements Traceability Matrix?

172. How will it affect the stakeholders personally in their career?

173. What is the WBS?

174. What percentage of Referral marketing projects are producing traceability matrices between requirements and other work products?

175. What are the chronologies, contingencies, consequences, criteria?

176. How do you manage scope?

177. Why do you manage scope?

178. How small is small enough?

179. Is there a requirements traceability process in place?

180. Describe the process for approving requirements so they can be added to the traceability matrix and Referral marketing project work can be performed. Will the Referral marketing project requirements

become approved in writing?

181. Why use a WBS?

2.6 Project Scope Statement: Referral marketing

182. Will an issue form be in use?

183. What are the major deliverables of the Referral marketing project?

184. Are the meetings set up to have assigned note takers that will add action/issues to the issue list?

185. Identify how your team and you will create the Referral marketing project scope statement and the work breakdown structure (WBS). Document how you will create the Referral marketing project scope statement and WBS, and make sure you answer the following questions: In defining Referral marketing project scope and the WBS, will you and your Referral marketing project team be using methods defined by your organization, methods defined by the Referral marketing project management office (PMO), or other methods?

186. Is your organization structure appropriate for the Referral marketing projects size and complexity?

187. Is the plan for your organization of the Referral marketing project resources adequate?

188. Have you been able to thoroughly document the Referral marketing projects assumptions and constraints?

189. Is the change control process documented and on file?

190. Are there completion/verification criteria defined for each task producing an output?

191. Change management vs. change leadership - what is the difference?

192. Write a brief purpose statement for this Referral marketing project. Include a business justification statement. What is the product of this Referral marketing project?

193. How will you haverify the accuracy of the work of the Referral marketing project, and what constitutes acceptance of the deliverables?

194. Which risks does the Referral marketing project focus on?

195. Have you been able to easily identify success criteria and create objective measurements for each of the Referral marketing project scopes goal statements?

196. How often will scope changes be reviewed?

197. Has the format for tracking and monitoring schedules and costs been defined?

198. Are there issues that could affect the existing requirements for the result, service, or product if the scope changes?

199. Any new risks introduced or old risks impacted.

Are there issues that could affect the existing requirements for the result, service, or product if the scope changes?

2.7 Assumption and Constraint Log: Referral marketing

200. Has the approach and development strategy of the Referral marketing project been defined, documented and accepted by the appropriate stakeholders?

201. Is the current scope of the Referral marketing project substantially different than that originally defined in the approved Referral marketing project plan?

202. Are there unnecessary steps that are creating bottlenecks and/or causing people to wait?

203. Does the Referral marketing project have a formal Referral marketing project Plan?

204. Have Referral marketing project management standards and procedures been established and documented?

205. Does the document/deliverable meet all requirements (for example, statement of work) specific to this deliverable?

206. What do you log?

207. Do the requirements meet the standards of correctness, completeness, consistency, accuracy, and readability?

208. Does the document/deliverable meet general requirements (for example, statement of work) for all deliverables?

209. If it is out of compliance, should the process be amended or should the Plan be amended?

210. Was the document/deliverable developed per the appropriate or required standards (for example, Institute of Electrical and Electronics Engineers standards)?

211. Are funding and staffing resource estimates sufficiently detailed and documented for use in planning and tracking the Referral marketing project?

212. Contradictory information between document sections?

213. Violation trace: why ?

214. Are requirements management tracking tools and procedures in place?

215. Are there cosmetic errors that hinder readability and comprehension?

216. What other teams / processes would be impacted by changes to the current process, and how?

217. Diagrams and tables are included to account for complex concepts and increase overall readability?

218. Are there processes in place to ensure internal consistency between the source code components?

219. Are there nonconformance issues?

2.8 Work Breakdown Structure: Referral marketing

220. Is it still viable?

221. Do you need another level?

222. How far down?

223. How big is a work-package?

224. What is the probability that the Referral marketing project duration will exceed xx weeks?

225. Where does it take place?

226. When do you stop?

227. How much detail?

228. Who has to do it?

229. Can you make it?

230. How will you and your Referral marketing project team define the Referral marketing projects scope and work breakdown structure?

231. Is the work breakdown structure (wbs) defined and is the scope of the Referral marketing project clear with assigned deliverable owners?

232. Why is it useful?

233. How many levels?

234. When would you develop a Work Breakdown Structure?

235. When does it have to be done?

236. Why would you develop a Work Breakdown Structure?

237. What is the probability of completing the Referral marketing project in less that xx days?

238. Is it a change in scope?

239. What has to be done?

2.9 WBS Dictionary: Referral marketing

240. Do work packages reflect the actual way in which the work will be done and are they meaningful products or management-oriented subdivisions of a higher level element of work?

241. Are time-phased budgets established for planning and control of level of effort activity by category of resource; for example, type of manpower and/or material?

242. Appropriate work authorization documents which subdivide the contractual effort and responsibilities, within functional organizations?

243. Is the work done on a work package level as described in the WBS dictionary?

244. Changes in the nature of the overhead requirements?

245. Are retroactive changes to BCWS and BCWP prohibited except for correction of errors or for normal accounting adjustments?

246. Software specification, development, integration, and testing, licenses ?

247. Does the contractor have procedures which permit identification of recurring or non-recurring costs as necessary?

248. Do work packages consist of discrete tasks which are adequately described?

249. Are the requirements for all items of overhead established by rational, traceable processes?

250. Are estimates of costs at completion utilized in determining contract funding requirements and reporting them?

251. Is all contract work included in the CWBS?

252. Are authorized changes being incorporated in a timely manner?

253. Does the cost accumulation system provide for summarization of indirect costs from the point of allocation to the contract total?

254. The anticipated business volume?

255. Authorization to proceed with all authorized work?

256. Are budgets or values assigned to work packages and planning packages in terms of dollars, hours, or other measurable units?

257. Is work properly classified as measured effort, LOE, or apportioned effort and appropriately separated?

258. Are procedures in existence that control replanning of unopened work packages, and are corresponding procedures adhered to?

2.10 Schedule Management Plan: Referral marketing

259. Has the scope management document been updated and distributed to help prevent scope creep?

260. How relevant is this attribute to this Referral marketing project or audit?

261. Are vendor invoices audited for accuracy before payment?

262. Why conduct schedule analysis?

263. Is there anything planned that does not need to be here?

264. Are vendor contract reports, reviews and visits conducted periodically?

265. Are meeting minutes captured and sent out after the meeting?

266. Are updated Referral marketing project time & resource estimates reasonable based on the current Referral marketing project stage?

267. Has your organization readiness assessment been conducted?

268. Was the scope definition used in task sequencing?

269. Sensitivity analysis?

270. Are metrics used to evaluate and manage Vendors?

271. Can be realistically shortened (the duration of subsequent tasks)?

272. Is there an onboarding process in place?

273. Are right task and resource calendars used in the IMS?

274. Are meeting objectives identified for each meeting?

275. Are the payment terms being followed?

276. Were the budget estimates reasonable?

2.11 Activity List: Referral marketing

277. When do the individual activities need to start and finish?

278. What went well?

279. What went right?

280. What did not go as well?

281. Is infrastructure setup part of your Referral marketing project?

282. For other activities, how much delay can be tolerated?

283. What are you counting on?

284. What is the LF and LS for each activity?

285. How do you determine the late start (LS) for each activity?

286. Where will it be performed?

287. How much slack is available in the Referral marketing project?

288. What are the critical bottleneck activities?

289. Should you include sub-activities?

290. How difficult will it be to do specific activities on

this Referral marketing project?

291. In what sequence?

292. How will it be performed?

293. When will the work be performed?

294. How can the Referral marketing project be displayed graphically to better visualize the activities?

2.12 Activity Attributes: Referral marketing

295. How do you manage time?

296. Would you consider either of corresponding activities an outlier?

297. Resources to accomplish the work?

298. Which method produces the more accurate cost assignment?

299. Are the required resources available?

300. How much activity detail is required?

301. Have you identified the Activity Leveling Priority code value on each activity?

302. Activity: what is In the Bag?

303. How else could the items be grouped?

304. Can more resources be added?

305. Were there other ways you could have organized the data to achieve similar results?

306. Does your organization of the data change its meaning?

307. Why?

308. How many resources do you need to complete the work scope within a limit of X number of days?

309. Where else does it apply?

310. Is there a trend during the year?

311. Has management defined a definite timeframe for the turnaround or Referral marketing project window?

312. Activity: fair or not fair?

2.13 Milestone List: Referral marketing

313. What would happen if a delivery of material was one week late?

314. What specific improvements did you make to the Referral marketing project proposal since the previous time?

315. What is the market for your technology, product or service?

316. Are the required resources available or need to be acquired?

317. Legislative effects?

318. Can you derive how soon can the whole Referral marketing project finish?

319. It is to be a narrative text providing the crucial aspects of your Referral marketing project proposal answering what, who, how, when and where?

320. How late can each activity be finished and started?

321. Reliability of data, plan predictability?

322. Political effects?

323. How difficult will it be to do specific activities on

this Referral marketing project?

324. Obstacles faced?

325. Sustaining internal capabilities?

326. Competitive advantages?

327. How soon can the activity finish?

328. Which path is the critical path?

329. Environmental effects?

330. Level of the Innovation?

2.14 Network Diagram: Referral marketing

331. Can you calculate the confidence level?

332. Are the gantt chart and/or network diagram updated periodically and used to assess the overall Referral marketing project timetable?

333. If a current contract exists, can you provide the vendor name, contract start, and contract expiration date?

334. What job or jobs follow it?

335. What are the Key Success Factors?

336. What is the lowest cost to complete this Referral marketing project in xx weeks?

337. Planning: who, how long, what to do?

338. What to do and When?

339. What is the completion time?

340. What job or jobs could run concurrently?

341. Where do schedules come from?

342. What activity must be completed immediately before this activity can start?

343. What controls the start and finish of a job?

344. Review the logical flow of the network diagram. Take a look at which activities you have first and then sequence the activities. Do they make sense?

345. How difficult will it be to do specific activities on this Referral marketing project?

346. What activities must occur simultaneously with this activity?

347. What is the probability of completing the Referral marketing project in less that xx days?

348. How confident can you be in your milestone dates and the delivery date?

2.15 Activity Resource Requirements: Referral marketing

349. Are there unresolved issues that need to be addressed?

350. Organizational Applicability?

351. Which logical relationship does the PDM use most often?

352. Other support in specific areas?

353. Anything else?

354. When does monitoring begin?

355. Why do you do that?

356. Do you use tools like decomposition and rolling-wave planning to produce the activity list and other outputs?

357. What are constraints that you might find during the Human Resource Planning process?

358. How do you handle petty cash?

359. What is the Work Plan Standard?

360. Time for overtime?

361. How many signatures do you require on a

check and does this match what is in your policy and procedures?

2.16 Resource Breakdown Structure: Referral marketing

362. Goals for the Referral marketing project. What is each stakeholders desired outcome for the Referral marketing project?

363. When do they need the information?

364. Who is allowed to perform which functions?

365. Is predictive resource analysis being done?

366. Why is this important?

367. What is the number one predictor of a groups productivity?

368. Who will use the system?

369. What is each stakeholders desired outcome for the Referral marketing project?

370. Why time management?

371. What defines a successful Referral marketing project?

372. How can this help you with team building?

373. What is the purpose of assigning and documenting responsibility?

374. What can you do to improve productivity?

375. Who will be used as a Referral marketing project team member?

376. What is the primary purpose of the human resource plan?

377. Any changes from stakeholders?

2.17 Activity Duration Estimates: Referral marketing

378. Is a work breakdown structure created to organize and to confirm the scope of each Referral marketing project?

379. Based on , if you need to shorten the duration of the Referral marketing project, what activity would you try to shorten?

380. Why is it difficult to use Referral marketing project management software well?

381. Does a process exist to determine which risk events to accept and which events to disregard?

382. What Referral marketing project was the first to use modern Referral marketing project management?

383. Research recruiting and retention strategies at three different companies. What distinguishes one organization from another in this area?

384. Are adjustments implemented to correct or prevent defects?

385. Which frame seemed to be the most important and why?

386. Are changes to the scope managed according to defined procedures?

387. What questions do you have about the sample documents provided?

388. Which would be the NEXT thing for the Referral marketing project manager to do?

389. Does a process exist to identify which qualified resources may be attainable?

390. Did anything besides luck make a difference between success and failure?

391. How does Referral marketing project integration management relate to the Referral marketing project life cycle, stakeholders, and the other Referral marketing project management knowledge areas?

392. Referral marketing project manager has received activity duration estimates from his team. Which does one need in order to complete schedule development?

393. What are the main parts of a scope statement?

394. What is the duration of a milestone?

395. Are procedures followed to ensure information is available to stakeholders in a timely manner?

396. Does the software appear easy to learn?

2.18 Duration Estimating Worksheet: Referral marketing

397. When does your organization expect to be able to complete it?

398. Small or large Referral marketing project?

399. When, then?

400. What utility impacts are there?

401. What is an Average Referral marketing project?

402. Why estimate costs?

403. Define the work as completely as possible. What work will be included in the Referral marketing project?

404. What info is needed?

405. Is the Referral marketing project responsive to community need?

406. What is cost and Referral marketing project cost management?

407. Is this operation cost effective?

408. How should ongoing costs be monitored to try to keep the Referral marketing project within budget?

409. What questions do you have?

410. Is a construction detail attached (to aid in explanation)?

411. Why estimate time and cost?

412. Done before proceeding with this activity or what can be done concurrently?

413. What is the total time required to complete the Referral marketing project if no delays occur?

2.19 Project Schedule: Referral marketing

414. Why do you need to manage Referral marketing project Risk?

415. Are there activities that came from a template or previous Referral marketing project that are not applicable on this phase of this Referral marketing project?

416. Did the Referral marketing project come in under budget?

417. Why do you think schedule issues often cause the most conflicts on Referral marketing projects?

418. Does the condition or event threaten the Referral marketing projects objectives in any ways?

419. Activity charts and bar charts are graphical representations of a Referral marketing project schedule ...how do they differ?

420. How can you fix it?

421. Did the Referral marketing project come in on schedule?

422. How do you use schedules?

423. Are quality inspections and review activities listed in the Referral marketing project schedule(s)?

424. If you can not fix it, how do you do it differently?

425. If there are any qualifying green components to this Referral marketing project, what portion of the total Referral marketing project cost is green?

426. Why is this particularly bad?

427. Is the structure for tracking the Referral marketing project schedule well defined and assigned to a specific individual?

428. Are you working on the right risks?

429. Verify that the update is accurate. Are all remaining durations correct?

430. How does a Referral marketing project get to be a year late ?

431. What is the difference?

432. Are key risk mitigation strategies added to the Referral marketing project schedule?

2.20 Cost Management Plan: Referral marketing

433. Are target dates established for each milestone deliverable?

434. Are all resource assumptions documented?

435. What is Referral marketing project management?

436. Are all vendor contracts closed out?

437. Is a pmo (Referral marketing project management office) in place and provide oversight to the Referral marketing project?

438. How do you manage cost?

439. Is it standard practice to formally commit stakeholders to the Referral marketing project via agreements?

440. Are corrective actions and variances reported?

441. Have reserves been created to address risks?

442. Is the structure for tracking the Referral marketing project schedule well defined and assigned to a specific individual?

443. Are risk oriented checklists used during risk identification?

444. What does this mean to a cost or scheduler manager?

445. Resources – how will human resources be scheduled during each phase of the Referral marketing project?

446. What is your organizations history in doing similar tasks?

447. How difficult will it be to do specific tasks on the Referral marketing project?

448. Does the resource management plan include a personnel development plan?

449. Are all payments made according to the contract(s)?

2.21 Activity Cost Estimates: Referral marketing

450. Does the estimator have experience?

451. How Award?

452. Is there anything unique in this Referral marketing projects scope statement that will affect resources?

453. How do you do activity recasts?

454. Padding is bad and contingencies are good. what is the difference?

455. What is the Referral marketing projects sustainability strategy that will ensure Referral marketing project results will endure or be sustained?

456. In which phase of the acquisition process cycle does source qualifications reside?

457. What were things that you did well, and could improve, and how?

458. Who & what determines the need for contracted services?

459. Will you use any tools, such as Referral marketing project management software, to assist in capturing Earned Value metrics?

460. Did the Referral marketing project team have the right skills?

461. What communication items need improvement?

462. What do you want to know about the stay to know if costs were inappropriately high or low?

463. Is costing method consistent with study goals?

464. How difficult will it be to do specific tasks on the Referral marketing project?

465. Based on your Referral marketing project communication management plan, what worked well?

466. Are data needed on characteristics of care?

467. Eac -estimate at completion, what is the total job expected to cost?

2.22 Cost Estimating Worksheet: Referral marketing

468. What additional Referral marketing project(s) could be initiated as a result of this Referral marketing project?

469. Value pocket identification & quantification what are value pockets?

470. How will the results be shared and to whom?

471. Can a trend be established from historical performance data on the selected measure and are the criteria for using trend analysis or forecasting methods met?

472. Is the Referral marketing project responsive to community need?

473. What costs are to be estimated?

474. What happens to any remaining funds not used?

475. Who is best positioned to know and assist in identifying corresponding factors?

476. What is the estimated labor cost today based upon this information?

477. Identify the timeframe necessary to monitor progress and collect data to determine how the selected measure has changed?

478. What is the purpose of estimating?

479. Will the Referral marketing project collaborate with the local community and leverage resources?

480. What can be included?

481. What will others want?

482. Is it feasible to establish a control group arrangement?

483. Does the Referral marketing project provide innovative ways for stakeholders to overcome obstacles or deliver better outcomes?

484. Ask: are others positioned to know, are others credible, and will others cooperate?

2.23 Cost Baseline: Referral marketing

485. How fast?

486. What weaknesses do you have?

487. What is the most important thing to do next to make your Referral marketing project successful?

488. Have you identified skills that are missing from your team?

489. Should a more thorough impact analysis be conducted?

490. Has the documentation relating to operation and maintenance of the product(s) or service(s) been delivered to, and accepted by, operations management?

491. Impact to environment?

492. What strengths do you have?

493. Has the actual cost of the Referral marketing project (or Referral marketing project phase) been tallied and compared to the approved budget?

494. Are there contingencies or conditions related to the acceptance?

495. Has the Referral marketing projected annual cost to operate and maintain the product(s) or service(s) been approved and funded?

496. At which frequency ?

497. Are you asking management for something as a result of this update?

498. Where do changes come from?

499. Have the actual milestone completion dates been compared to the approved schedule?

500. Has the Referral marketing project documentation been archived or otherwise disposed as described in the Referral marketing project communication plan?

501. What can go wrong?

502. How difficult will it be to do specific tasks on the Referral marketing project?

2.24 Quality Management Plan: Referral marketing

503. How does your organization establish and maintain customer relationships?

504. Are formal code reviews conducted?

505. Documented results available?

506. What is quality planning ?

507. What would you gain if you spent time working to improve this process?

508. How are training records kept?

509. After observing execution of process, is it in compliance with the documented Plan?

510. How do you ensure that your sampling methods and procedures meet your data needs?

511. How relevant is this attribute to this Referral marketing project or audit?

512. Was trending evident between audits?

513. Does the Referral marketing project have a formal Referral marketing project Plan?

514. Show/provide copy of procedures for taking field notes?

515. Have all necessary approvals been obtained?

516. Is the amount of effort justified by the anticipated value of forming a new process?

517. What are your key performance measures/indicators for tracking progress relative to your action plans?

518. Have you eliminated all duplicative tasks or manual efforts, where appropriate?

519. Was trending evident between reviews?

520. How do you document and correct nonconformances?

521. Can you perform this task or activity in a more effective manner?

522. Checking the completeness and appropriateness of the sampling and testing. Were the right locations/samples tested for the right parameters?

2.25 Quality Metrics: Referral marketing

523. Have alternatives been defined in the event that failure occurs?

524. What are your organizations expectations for its quality Referral marketing project?

525. Who notifies stakeholders of normal and abnormal results?

526. Who is willing to lead?

527. Are quality metrics defined?

528. Has risk analysis been adequately reviewed?

529. Which data do others need in one place to target areas of improvement?

530. What happens if you get an abnormal result?

531. Are applicable standards referenced and available?

532. Is material complete (and does it meet the standards)?

533. If the defect rate during testing is substantially higher than that of the previous release (or a similar product), then ask: Did you plan for and actually improve testing effectiveness?

534. What documentation is required?

535. Did the team meet the Referral marketing project success criteria documented in the Quality Metrics Matrix?

536. Can visual measures help you to filter visualizations of interest?

537. How does one achieve stability?

538. Do you know how much profit a 10% decrease in waste would generate?

539. Is there alignment within your organization on definitions?

540. Is there a set of procedures to capture, analyze and act on quality metrics?

541. Subjective quality component: customer satisfaction, how do you measure it?

542. What group is empowered to define quality requirements?

2.26 Process Improvement Plan: Referral marketing

543. What is the test-cycle concept?

544. Where are you now?

545. Are there forms and procedures to collect and record the data?

546. Are you meeting the quality standards?

547. Why quality management?

548. Everyone agrees on what process improvement is, right?

549. How do you manage quality?

550. Has the time line required to move measurement results from the points of collection to databases or users been established?

551. What personnel are the coaches for your initiative?

552. Are you making progress on the improvement framework?

553. To elicit goal statements, do you ask a question such as, What do you want to achieve?

554. Purpose of goal: the motive is determined by

asking, why do you want to achieve this goal?

555. Where do you focus?

556. Are you making progress on the goals?

557. What makes people good SPI coaches?

558. What lessons have you learned so far?

559. What actions are needed to address the problems and achieve the goals?

560. Management commitment at all levels?

561. Does explicit definition of the measures exist?

562. Are you following the quality standards?

2.27 Responsibility Assignment Matrix: Referral marketing

563. Are records maintained to show how management reserves are used?

564. Who is going to do that work?

565. What does wbs accomplish?

566. How many hours by each staff member/rate?

567. Is it safe to say you can handle more work or that some tasks you are supposed to do arent worth doing?

568. What will the work cost?

569. Detailed schedules which support control account and work package start and completion dates/events?

570. Are there any drawbacks to using a responsibility assignment matrix?

571. Are records maintained to show how undistributed budgets are controlled?

572. Are your organizations and items of cost assigned to each pool identified?

573. The staff characteristics – is the group or the person capable to work together as a team?

574. What happens when others get pulled for higher priority Referral marketing projects?

575. Do you need to convince people that its well worth the time and effort?

576. Changes in the direct base to which overhead costs are allocated?

577. Are overhead cost budgets established for each organization which has authority to incur overhead costs?

578. Are others working on the right things?

2.28 Roles and Responsibilities: Referral marketing

579. Concern: where are you limited or have no authority, where you can not influence?

580. Key conclusions and recommendations: Are conclusions and recommendations relevant and acceptable?

581. Are your budgets supportive of a culture of quality data?

582. Be specific; avoid generalities. Thank you and great work alone are insufficient. What exactly do you appreciate and why?

583. To decide whether to use a quality measurement, ask how will you know when it is achieved?

584. What expectations were NOT met?

585. Once the responsibilities are defined for the Referral marketing project, have the deliverables, roles and responsibilities been clearly communicated to every participant?

586. Who is responsible for each task?

587. How well did the Referral marketing project Team understand the expectations of specific roles and responsibilities?

588. Who is involved?

589. What should you do now to prepare for your career 5+ years from now?

590. How is your work-life balance?

591. Accountabilities: what are the roles and responsibilities of individual team members?

592. What is working well within your organizations performance management system?

593. Does your vision/mission support a culture of quality data?

594. Are Referral marketing project team roles and responsibilities identified and documented?

595. What should you highlight for improvement?

596. Influence: what areas of organizational decision making are you able to influence when you do not have authority to make the final decision?

597. Are Referral marketing project team roles and responsibilities identified and documented?

598. Attainable / achievable: the goal is attainable; can you actually accomplish the goal?

2.29 Human Resource Management Plan: Referral marketing

599. Were stakeholders aware and supportive of the principles and practices of modern cost estimation?

600. Who needs training?

601. Are post milestone Referral marketing project reviews (PMPR) conducted with your organization at least once a year?

602. Is the schedule updated on a periodic basis?

603. Identify who is needed on the core Referral marketing project team to complete Referral marketing project deliverables and achieve its goals and objectives. What skills, knowledge and experiences are required?

604. Specific - is the objective clear in terms of what, how, when, and where the situation will be changed?

605. Have process improvement efforts been completed before requirements efforts begin?

606. Do people have the competencies to meet the strategic objectives?

607. Is there a set of procedures defining the scope, procedures, and deliverables defining quality control?

608. Are multiple estimation methods being

employed?

609. Are enough systems & user personnel assigned to the Referral marketing project?

610. Have stakeholder accountabilities & responsibilities been clearly defined?

611. Has the business need been clearly defined?

612. Are people motivated to meet the current and future challenges?

613. Is the manpower level sufficient to meet the future business requirements?

614. Who is evaluated?

615. Are the Referral marketing project plans updated on a frequent basis?

2.30 Communications Management Plan: Referral marketing

616. What data is going to be required?

617. How were corresponding initiatives successful?

618. Who have you worked with in past, similar initiatives?

619. Do you ask; can you recommend others for you to talk with about this initiative?

620. Who will use or be affected by the result of a Referral marketing project?

621. Who is involved as you identify stakeholders?

622. What to learn?

623. Conflict resolution -which method when?

624. Why do you manage communications?

625. Are you constantly rushing from meeting to meeting?

626. Are there common objectives between the team and the stakeholder?

627. Are stakeholders internal or external?

628. Who to share with?

629. How is this initiative related to other portfolios, programs, or Referral marketing projects?

630. Why is stakeholder engagement important?

631. What are the interrelationships?

632. What approaches do you use?

633. Do you feel more overwhelmed by stakeholders?

634. Who is responsible?

635. How often do you engage with stakeholders?

2.31 Risk Management Plan: Referral marketing

636. What can you do to minimize the impact if it does?

637. Workarounds are determined during which step of risk management?

638. Was an original risk assessment/risk management plan completed?

639. Could others have been better mitigated?

640. What risks are tracked?

641. What things are likely to change?

642. What is the cost to the Referral marketing project if it does occur?

643. Prioritized components/features?

644. Why is product liability a serious issue?

645. Technology risk: is the Referral marketing project technically feasible?

646. Are tools for analysis and design available?

647. Are there risks to human health or the environment that need to be controlled or mitigated?

648. Are there new risks that mitigation strategies might introduce?

649. How well were you able to manage your risk before?

650. Minimize cost and financial risk?

651. Maximize short-term return on investment?

652. My Referral marketing project leader has suddenly left your organization, what do you do?

653. How quickly does this item need to be resolved?

2.32 Risk Register: Referral marketing

654. What could prevent you delivering on the strategic program objectives and what is being done to mitigate corresponding issues?

655. Does the evidence highlight any areas to advance opportunities or foster good relations. If yes what steps will be taken?

656. What is a Risk?

657. Manageability – have mitigations to the risk been identified?

658. How could corresponding Risk affect the Referral marketing project in terms of cost and schedule?

659. What would the impact to the Referral marketing project objectives be should the risk arise?

660. Do you require further engagement?

661. Which key risks have ineffective responses or outstanding improvement actions?

662. People risk -are people with appropriate skills available to help complete the Referral marketing project?

663. Recovery actions - planned actions taken once a risk has occurred to allow you to move on. What should you do after?

664. Are there any gaps in the evidence?

665. What are the main aims, objectives of the policy, strategy, or service and the intended outcomes?

666. What are the major risks facing the Referral marketing project?

667. Why would you develop a risk register?

668. How are risks graded?

669. What are you going to do to limit the Referral marketing projects risk exposure due to the identified risks?

670. Amongst the action plans and recommendations that you have to introduce are there some that could stop or delay the overall program?

671. When would you develop a risk register?

672. Risk documentation: what reporting formats and processes will be used for risk management activities?

673. What action, if any, has been taken to respond to the risk?

2.33 Probability and Impact Assessment: Referral marketing

674. What are the preparations required for facing difficulties?

675. What are the chances the risk event will occur?

676. Have staff received necessary training?

677. How completely has the customer been identified?

678. Why has this particular mode of contracting been chosen?

679. What should be the external organizations responsibility vis-à-vis total stake in the Referral marketing project?

680. Are testing tools available and suitable?

681. What risks are necessary to achieve success?

682. When and how will the recent breakthroughs in basic research lead to commercial products?

683. Is the number of people on the Referral marketing project team adequate to do the job?

684. Risk urgency assessment -which of your risks could occur soon, or require a longer planning time?

685. Mitigation -how can you avoid the risk?

686. What will be the likely political environment during the life of the Referral marketing project?

687. What is the experience (performance, attitude, business ethics, etc.) in the past with contractors?

688. What are the current or emerging trends of culture?

689. Are enough people available?

690. Are there any Referral marketing projects similar to this one in existence?

691. What are the tools and techniques used in managing the challenges faced?

692. Does the software interface with new or unproven hardware or unproven vendor products?

2.34 Probability and Impact Matrix: Referral marketing

693. What changes in the regulation are forthcoming?

694. What things might go wrong?

695. Do you have specific methods that you use for each phase of the process?

696. Is a software Referral marketing project management tool available?

697. Mandated specific features?

698. What is the risk appetite?

699. How solid are the price-volume Referral marketing projections?

700. Are some people working on multiple Referral marketing projects?

701. Economic to take on the Referral marketing project?

702. Management -what contingency plans do you have if the risk becomes a reality?

703. Is the technology to be built new to your organization?

704. How are you working with risks?

705. What would be the effect of slippage?

706. Are staff committed for the duration of the Referral marketing project?

707. Non-valid or incredible information?

708. What is the likelihood of a breakthrough?

709. Do you manage the process through use of metrics?

2.35 Risk Data Sheet: Referral marketing

710. What was measured?

711. How can hazards be reduced?

712. What are you trying to achieve (Objectives)?

713. What are you weak at and therefore need to do better?

714. What is the duration of infection (the length of time the host is infected with the organizm) in a normal healthy human host?

715. How do you handle product safely?

716. Do effective diagnostic tests exist?

717. During work activities could hazards exist?

718. What were the Causes that contributed?

719. Has the most cost-effective solution been chosen?

720. Who has a vested interest in how you perform as your organization (our stakeholders)?

721. What is the environment within which you operate (social trends, economic, community values, broad based participation, national directions etc.)?

722. Are new hazards created?

723. Risk of what?

724. What do people affected think about the need for, and practicality of preventive measures?

725. How reliable is the data source?

726. What are the main threats to your existence?

727. What is the likelihood of it happening?

728. Whom do you serve (customers)?

729. What actions can be taken to eliminate or remove risk?

2.36 Procurement Management Plan: Referral marketing

730. What is a Referral marketing project Management Plan?

731. Why is procurement planning important?

732. Are estimating assumptions and constraints captured?

733. How will the duration of the Referral marketing project influence your decisions?

734. Were Referral marketing project team members involved in detailed estimating and scheduling?

735. How will you coordinate Procurement with aspects of the Referral marketing project?

736. Are enough systems & user personnel assigned to the Referral marketing project?

737. Are changes in deliverable commitments agreed to by all affected groups & individuals?

738. Are risk triggers captured?

739. Are non-critical path items updated and agreed upon with the teams?

2.37 Source Selection Criteria: Referral marketing

740. What can not be disclosed?

741. What is the role of counsel in the procurement process?

742. What are the most common types of rating systems?

743. What documentation should be used to support the selection decision?

744. What risks were identified in the proposals?

745. How are oral presentations documented?

746. How are clarifications and communications appropriately used?

747. How much weight should be placed on past performance information?

748. What should be considered when developing evaluation standards?

749. Are types/quantities of material, facilities appropriate?

750. How can solicitation Schedules be improved to yield more effective price competition?

751. How should oral presentations be prepared for?

752. What should a DRFP include?

753. Does your documentation identify why the team concurs or differs with reported performance from past performance report (CPARs, questionnaire responses, etc.)?

754. Are there any common areas of weaknesses or deficiencies in the proposals in the competitive range?

755. How should the solicitation aspects regarding past performance be structured?

756. Why promote competition?

757. Do you prepare an independent cost estimate?

758. Do you have designated specific forms or worksheets?

759. What should be the contracting officers strategy?

2.38 Stakeholder Management Plan: Referral marketing

760. Does the Referral marketing project have a formal Referral marketing project Plan?

761. Who will be collecting information?

762. Is staff trained on the software technologies that are being used on the Referral marketing project?

763. Have the key elements of a coherent Referral marketing project management strategy been established?

764. Why would a customer be interested in a particular product or service?

765. Have the key functions and capabilities been defined and assigned to each release or iteration?

766. Is the current scope of the Referral marketing project substantially different than that originally defined?

767. Are actuals compared against estimates to analyze and correct variances?

768. Are the schedule estimates reasonable given the Referral marketing project?

769. Have all documents been archived in a Referral marketing project repository for each release?

770. In your opinion, do certain Referral marketing project resources hold a higher importance than other resources?

771. Are there any potential occupational health and safety issues due to the proposed purchases?

772. Is there any form of automated support for Issues Management?

2.39 Change Management Plan: Referral marketing

773. What are the specific target groups/audiences that will be impacted by this change?

774. What new behaviours are required?

775. What roles within your organization are affected, and how?

776. Has the target training audience been identified and nominated?

777. Why would a Referral marketing project run more smoothly when change management is emphasized from the beginning?

778. How much change management is needed?

779. What are you trying to achieve as a result of communication?

780. What are the essentials of the message?

781. Who will fund the training?

782. What are the specific target groups / audience that will be impacted by this change?

783. Who might be able to help you the most?

784. Which relationships will change?

785. Have the approved procedures and policies been published?

786. Will a different work structure focus people on what is important?

787. What communication network would you use – informal or formal?

788. Who is responsible for which tasks?

789. What policies and procedures need to be changed?

790. What are the current methods of sharing information and do there need to be new ones developed?

791. Identify the current level of skills and knowledge and behaviours of the group that will be impacted on. What prerequisite knowledge do corresponding groups need?

792. Identify the risk and assess the significance and likelihood of it occurring and plan the contingency What risks may occur upfront?

3.0 Executing Process Group: Referral marketing

793. What is the shortest possible time it will take to complete this Referral marketing project?

794. Mitigate. what will you do to minimize the impact should a risk event occur?

795. What are the key components of the Referral marketing project communications plan?

796. Does the Referral marketing project team have enough people to execute the Referral marketing project plan?

797. If a risk event occurs, what will you do?

798. How will you avoid scope creep?

799. Could a new application negatively affect the current IT infrastructure?

800. Who will provide training?

801. Does software appear easy to learn?

802. Contingency planning. if a risk event occurs, what will you do?

803. What areas does the group agree are the biggest success on the Referral marketing project?

804. What areas were overlooked on this Referral marketing project?

805. Do Referral marketing project managers understand your organizational context for Referral marketing projects?

806. How do you enter durations, link tasks, and view critical path information?

807. What is in place for ensuring adequate change control on Referral marketing projects that involve outside contracts?

808. What is involved in the solicitation process?

809. Do the partners have sufficient financial capacity to keep up the benefits produced by the programme?

3.1 Team Member Status Report: Referral marketing

810. How does this product, good, or service meet the needs of the Referral marketing project and your organization as a whole?

811. How it is to be done?

812. Does the product, good, or service already exist within your organization?

813. Will the staff do training or is that done by a third party?

814. When a teams productivity and success depend on collaboration and the efficient flow of information, what generally fails them?

815. How will resource planning be done?

816. How can you make it practical?

817. How much risk is involved?

818. Is there evidence that staff is taking a more professional approach toward management of your organizations Referral marketing projects?

819. Does every department have to have a Referral marketing project Manager on staff?

820. What specific interest groups do you have in

place?

821. The problem with Reward & Recognition Programs is that the truly deserving people all too often get left out. How can you make it practical?

822. What is to be done?

823. Are the products of your organizations Referral marketing projects meeting customers objectives?

824. Why is it to be done?

825. Do you have an Enterprise Referral marketing project Management Office (EPMO)?

826. Does your organization have the means (staff, money, contract, etc.) to produce or to acquire the product, good, or service?

827. Are the attitudes of staff regarding Referral marketing project work improving?

828. Are your organizations Referral marketing projects more successful over time?

3.2 Change Request: Referral marketing

829. What type of changes does change control take into account?

830. Has a formal technical review been conducted to assess technical correctness?

831. How well do experienced software developers predict software change?

832. Are you implementing itil processes?

833. How many lines of code must be changed to implement the change?

834. Change request coordination ?

835. What are the Impacts to your organization?

836. What needs to be communicated?

837. Can static requirements change attributes like the size of the change be used to predict reliability in execution?

838. How are the measures for carrying out the change established?

839. Who is communicating the change?

840. How do team members communicate with each

other?

841. How shall the implementation of changes be recorded?

842. How can changes be graded?

843. Will this change conflict with other requirements changes (e.g., lead to conflicting operational scenarios)?

844. What must be taken into consideration when introducing change control programs?

845. Screen shots or attachments included in a Change Request?

846. Why were your requested changes rejected or not made?

847. Who can suggest changes?

848. How many times must the change be modified or presented to the change control board before it is approved?

3.3 Change Log: Referral marketing

849. Is the change backward compatible without limitations?

850. Is the change request open, closed or pending?

851. Is the change request within Referral marketing project scope?

852. Do the described changes impact on the integrity or security of the system?

853. How does this change affect scope?

854. Is the submitted change a new change or a modification of a previously approved change?

855. How does this change affect the timeline of the schedule?

856. When was the request approved?

857. Will the Referral marketing project fail if the change request is not executed?

858. Is this a mandatory replacement?

859. Does the suggested change request seem to represent a necessary enhancement to the product?

860. Who initiated the change request?

861. How does this relate to the standards developed

for specific business processes?

862. Is the requested change request a result of changes in other Referral marketing project(s)?

863. Does the suggested change request represent a desired enhancement to the products functionality?

864. When was the request submitted?

3.4 Decision Log: Referral marketing

865. How effective is maintaining the log at facilitating organizational learning?

866. How do you know when you are achieving it?

867. Does anything need to be adjusted?

868. Meeting purpose; why does this team meet?

869. What is the line where eDiscovery ends and document review begins?

870. Who will be given a copy of this document and where will it be kept?

871. Who is the decisionmaker?

872. How does the use a Decision Support System influence the strategies/tactics or costs?

873. What is your overall strategy for quality control / quality assurance procedures?

874. How does an increasing emphasis on cost containment influence the strategies and tactics used?

875. Adversarial environment. is your opponent open to a non-traditional workflow, or will it likely challenge anything you do?

876. Linked to original objective?

877. What was the rationale for the decision?

878. How consolidated and comprehensive a story can you tell by capturing currently available incident data in a central location and through a log of key decisions during an incident?

879. Behaviors; what are guidelines that the team has identified that will assist them with getting the most out of team meetings?

880. How does provision of information, both in terms of content and presentation, influence acceptance of alternative strategies?

881. Is everything working as expected?

882. Which variables make a critical difference?

883. How do you define success?

884. Decision-making process; how will the team make decisions?

3.5 Quality Audit: Referral marketing

885. How does your organization know that its system for recruiting the best staff possible are appropriately effective and constructive?

886. What is the collective experience of the team to be assigned to an audit?

887. What review processes are in place for your organizations major activities?

888. Are all records associated with the reconditioning of a device maintained for a minimum of two years after the sale or disposal of the last device within a lot of merchandise?

889. How does your organization know that its system for managing intellectual property issues is appropriately effective, constructive and fair?

890. How does your organization know that its quality of teaching is appropriately effective and constructive?

891. How does your organization know that its advisory services are appropriately effective and constructive?

892. Do the suppliers use a formal quality system?

893. How does your organization know that its research programs are appropriately effective and constructive?

894. How does your organization know that it is effectively and constructively guiding staff through to timely completion of tasks?

895. What does the organizarion look for in a Quality audit?

896. Are all employees made aware of device defects which may occur from the improper performance of specific jobs?

897. Are there appropriate means for intervening if necessary?

898. How does your organization know that its systems for providing high quality consultancy services to external parties are appropriately effective and constructive?

899. How does your organization know that its system for attending to the particular needs of its international staff is appropriately effective and constructive?

900. Has a written procedure been established to identify devices during all stages of receipt, reconditioning, distribution and installation so that mix-ups are prevented?

901. How does your organization know that its information technology system is serving its needs as effectively and constructively as is appropriate?

902. How does your organization know that its system for governing staff behaviour is appropriately

effective and constructive?

903. Are multiple statements on the same issue consistent with each other?

904. For each device to be reconditioned, are device specifications, such as appropriate engineering drawings, component specifications and software specifications, maintained?

3.6 Team Directory: Referral marketing

905. Who should receive information (all stakeholders)?

906. Who are the Team Members?

907. Who will be the stakeholders on your next Referral marketing project?

908. Who is the Sponsor?

909. Have you decided when to celebrate the Referral marketing projects completion date?

910. Do purchase specifications and configurations match requirements?

911. Does a Referral marketing project team directory list all resources assigned to the Referral marketing project?

912. Contract requirements complied with?

913. How and in what format should information be presented?

914. Timing: when do the effects of communication take place?

915. Process decisions: are contractors adequately prosecuting the work?

916. Process decisions: do job conditions warrant additional actions to collect job information and document on-site activity?

917. Decisions: is the most suitable form of contract being used?

918. Decisions: what could be done better to improve the quality of the constructed product?

919. Is construction on schedule?

920. Where should the information be distributed?

921. How does the team resolve conflicts and ensure tasks are completed?

922. Where will the product be used and/or delivered or built when appropriate?

923. Why is the work necessary?

3.7 Team Operating Agreement: Referral marketing

924. Communication protocols: how will the team communicate?

925. Are there differences in access to communication and collaboration technology based on team member location?

926. Seconds for members to respond?

927. What is culture?

928. What is a Virtual Team?

929. Do you ask participants to close laptops and place mobile devices on silent on the table while the meeting is in progress?

930. Must your team members rely on the expertise of other members to complete tasks?

931. What is your unique contribution to your organization?

932. To whom do you deliver your services?

933. Do team members reside in more than two countries?

934. Are leadership responsibilities shared among team members (versus a single leader)?

935. Resource allocation: how will individual team members account for time and expenses, and how will this be allocated in the team budget?

936. Are there more than two national cultures represented by your team?

937. Do you use a parking lot for any items that are important and outside of the agenda?

938. Do you record meetings for the already stated unable to attend?

939. Are there influences outside the team that may affect performance, and if so, have you identified and addressed them?

940. Do you post any action items, due dates, and responsibilities on the team website?

941. Do you send out the agenda and meeting materials in advance?

942. Do you listen for voice tone and word choice to understand the meaning behind words?

943. Did you draft the meeting agenda?

3.8 Team Performance Assessment: Referral marketing

944. To what degree are the teams goals and objectives clear, simple, and measurable?

945. How does Referral marketing project termination impact Referral marketing project team members?

946. To what degree can team members frequently and easily communicate with one another?

947. What are teams?

948. To what degree are corresponding categories of skills either actually or potentially represented across the membership?

949. To what degree do team members frequently explore the teams purpose and its implications?

950. Effects of crew composition on crew performance: Does the whole equal the sum of its parts?

951. To what degree are the goals ambitious?

952. To what degree can team members meet frequently enough to accomplish the teams ends?

953. To what degree will the team ensure that all members equitably share the work essential to the success of the team?

954. To what degree are fresh input and perspectives systematically caught and added (for example, through information and analysis, new members, and senior sponsors)?

955. To what degree will new and supplemental skills be introduced as the need is recognized?

956. To what degree does the team possess adequate membership to achieve its ends?

957. To what degree do the goals specify concrete team work products?

958. What are you doing specifically to develop the leaders around you?

959. To what degree is there a sense that only the team can succeed?

960. Where to from here?

961. To what degree does the teams approach to its work allow for modification and improvement over time?

962. What do you think is the most constructive thing that could be done now to resolve considerations and disputes about method variance?

963. Can familiarity breed backup?

3.9 Team Member Performance Assessment: Referral marketing

964. To what degree are the skill areas critical to team performance present?

965. How do you currently account for your results in the teams achievement?

966. To what extent are systems and applications (e.g., game engine, mobile device platform) utilized?

967. How do you use data to inform instruction and improve staff achievement?

968. What qualities does a successful Team leader possess?

969. What resources do you need?

970. To what degree are the relative importance and priority of the goals clear to all team members?

971. How is the timing of assessments organized (e.g., pre/post-test, single point during training, multiple reassessment during training)?

972. How are training activities developed from a technical perspective?

973. To what degree can the team measure progress against specific goals?

974. How do you currently use the time that is available?

975. How is assessment information achieved, stored?

976. Are assessment validation activities performed?

977. In what areas would you like to concentrate your knowledge and resources?

978. What variables that affect team members achievement are within your control?

979. To what degree are the goals realistic?

980. What instructional strategies were developed/ incorporated (e.g., direct instruction, indirect instruction, experiential learning, independent study, interactive instruction)?

3.10 Issue Log: Referral marketing

981. What help do you and your team need from the stakeholders?

982. Are the Referral marketing project issues uniquely identified, including to which product they refer?

983. Which stakeholders can influence others?

984. How were past initiatives successful?

985. Do you often overlook a key stakeholder or stakeholder group?

986. How much time does it take to do it?

987. Do you have members of your team responsible for certain stakeholders?

988. What approaches to you feel are the best ones to use?

989. Can you think of other people who might have concerns or interests?

990. Is the issue log kept in a safe place?

991. How do you reply to this question; you am new here and managing this major program. How do you suggest you build your network?

992. Who reported the issue?

993. Who are the members of the governing body?

994. What is a change?

995. What are the stakeholders interrelationships?

996. What steps can you take for positive relationships?

4.0 Monitoring and Controlling Process Group: Referral marketing

997. What is the timeline?

998. What kinds of things in particular are you looking for data on?

999. Is it what was agreed upon?

1000. Did the Referral marketing project team have enough people to execute the Referral marketing project plan?

1001. Is the verbiage used appropriate and understandable?

1002. How will staff learn how to use the deliverables?

1003. What resources (both financial and non-financial) are available/needed?

1004. Is progress on outcomes due to your program?

1005. How can you make your needs known?

1006. Accuracy: what design will lead to accurate information?

1007. Purpose: toward what end is the evaluation being conducted?

1008. Change, where should you look for problems?

1009. How to ensure validity, quality and consistency?

1010. Were decisions made in a timely manner?

1011. How is agile portfolio management done?

1012. How well did the team follow the chosen processes?

1013. Feasibility: how much money, time, and effort can you put into this?

1014. Just how important is your work to the overall success of the Referral marketing project?

1015. What were things that you did very well and want to do the same again on the next Referral marketing project?

4.1 Project Performance Report: Referral marketing

1016. To what degree does the formal organization make use of individual resources and meet individual needs?

1017. To what degree are the tasks requirements reflected in the flow and storage of information?

1018. How will procurement be coordinated with other Referral marketing project aspects, such as scheduling and performance reporting?

1019. To what degree does the teams work approach provide opportunity for members to engage in fact-based problem solving?

1020. What is the PRS?

1021. To what degree can team members vigorously define the teams purpose in considerations with others who are not part of the functioning team?

1022. To what degree do members articulate the goals beyond the team membership?

1023. What is the degree to which rules govern information exchange between groups?

1024. To what degree does the information network provide individuals with the information they require?

1025. To what degree do team members understand one anothers roles and skills?

1026. To what degree does the teams purpose contain themes that are particularly meaningful and memorable?

1027. To what degree is the team cognizant of small wins to be celebrated along the way?

1028. To what degree do team members feel that the purpose of the team is important, if not exciting?

1029. To what degree does the teams work approach provide opportunity for members to engage in open interaction?

1030. To what degree do all members feel responsible for all agreed-upon measures?

1031. To what degree are the demands of the task compatible with and converge with the relationships of the informal organization?

4.2 Variance Analysis: Referral marketing

1032. Are the wbs and organizational levels for application of the Referral marketing projected overhead costs identified?

1033. What is your organizations rationale for sharing expenses and services between business segments?

1034. Can process improvements lead to unfavorable variances?

1035. Other relevant issues of Variance Analysis -selling price or gross margin?

1036. What does a favorable labor efficiency variance mean?

1037. Are the overhead pools formally and adequately identified?

1038. Do you identify potential or actual budget-based and time-based schedule variances?

1039. Are overhead costs budgets established on a basis consistent with the anticipated direct business base?

1040. How do you identify potential or actual overruns and underruns?

1041. Who is generally responsible for monitoring and

taking action on variances?

1042. Does the accounting system provide a basis for auditing records of direct costs chargeable to the contract?

1043. Is budgeted cost for work performed calculated in a manner consistent with the way work is planned?

1044. Why do variances exist?

1045. How does your organization measure performance?

1046. Who are responsible for overhead performance control of related costs?

1047. Does the contractor use objective results, design reviews and tests to trace schedule performance?

1048. Wbs elements contractually specified for reporting of status to your organization (lowest level only)?

1049. Are all elements of indirect expense identified to overhead cost budgets of Referral marketing projections?

1050. How do you haverify authorization to proceed with all authorized work?

1051. What is the performance to date and material commitment?

4.3 Earned Value Status: Referral marketing

1052. Are you hitting your Referral marketing projects targets?

1053. Validation is a process of ensuring that the developed system will actually achieve the stakeholders desired outcomes; Are you building the right product? What do you validate?

1054. If earned value management (EVM) is so good in determining the true status of a Referral marketing project and Referral marketing project its completion, why is it that hardly any one uses it in information systems related Referral marketing projects?

1055. How much is it going to cost by the finish?

1056. Verification is a process of ensuring that the developed system satisfies the stakeholders agreements and specifications; Are you building the product right? What do you haverify?

1057. What is the unit of forecast value?

1058. Earned value can be used in almost any Referral marketing project situation and in almost any Referral marketing project environment. it may be used on large Referral marketing projects, medium sized Referral marketing projects, tiny Referral marketing projects (in cut-down form), complex and simple Referral marketing projects and in any market sector.

some people, of course, know all about earned value, they have used it for years - but perhaps not as effectively as they could have?

1059. When is it going to finish?

1060. How does this compare with other Referral marketing projects?

1061. Where are your problem areas?

1062. Where is evidence-based earned value in your organization reported?

4.4 Risk Audit: Referral marketing

1063. Are contracts reviewed before renewal?

1064. Does the customer understand the process?

1065. Do you conduct risk assessments on all programs, activities and events?

1066. Does your auditor understand your business?

1067. Where will the next scandal or adverse media involving your organization come from?

1068. Do you record and file all audits?

1069. Do industry specialists and business risk auditors enhance audit reporting accuracy?

1070. Whence the business risk audit?

1071. Estimated size of product in number of programs, files, transactions?

1072. When your organization is entering into a major contract, does it seek legal advice?

1073. What are the commonly used work arounds in high risk areas?

1074. What is the implication of budget constraint on this process?

1075. To what extent are auditors influenced by

the business risk assessment in the audit process, and how can auditors create more effective mental models to more fully examine contradictory evidence?

1076. Have permissions or required permits to use facilities managed by other parties been obtained?

1077. Level of preparation and skill?

1078. Do the people have the right combinations of skills?

1079. What compliance systems do you have in place to address quality, errors, and outcomes?

1080. What impact does prior experience have on decisions made during the risk-assessment process?

1081. Are corresponding safety and risk management policies posted for all to see?

1082. Have reasonable steps been taken to reduce the risks to acceptable levels?

4.5 Contractor Status Report: Referral marketing

1083. How does the proposed individual meet each requirement?

1084. Are there contractual transfer concerns?

1085. What was the final actual cost?

1086. What was the overall budget or estimated cost?

1087. Who can list a Referral marketing project as organization experience, your organization or a previous employee of your organization?

1088. How long have you been using the services?

1089. What are the minimum and optimal bandwidth requirements for the proposed soluiton?

1090. What process manages the contracts?

1091. How is risk transferred?

1092. What was the actual budget or estimated cost for your organizations services?

1093. Describe how often regular updates are made to the proposed solution. Are corresponding regular updates included in the standard maintenance plan?

1094. If applicable; describe your standard schedule

for new software version releases. Are new software version releases included in the standard maintenance plan?

1095. What was the budget or estimated cost for your organizations services?

1096. What is the average response time for answering a support call?

4.6 Formal Acceptance: Referral marketing

1097. Did the Referral marketing project manager and team act in a professional and ethical manner?

1098. Was the Referral marketing project managed well?

1099. Who would use it?

1100. Was the sponsor/customer satisfied?

1101. What are the requirements against which to test, Who will execute?

1102. Do you perform formal acceptance or burn-in tests?

1103. What is the Acceptance Management Process?

1104. Does it do what Referral marketing project team said it would?

1105. General estimate of the costs and times to complete the Referral marketing project?

1106. Was the Referral marketing project work done on time, within budget, and according to specification?

1107. How does your team plan to obtain formal acceptance on your Referral marketing project?

1108. Do you buy-in installation services?

1109. Have all comments been addressed?

1110. Do you buy pre-configured systems or build your own configuration?

1111. Was the Referral marketing project goal achieved?

1112. What function(s) does it fill or meet?

1113. What was done right?

1114. What can you do better next time?

1115. What features, practices, and processes proved to be strengths or weaknesses?

1116. Was business value realized?

5.0 Closing Process Group: Referral marketing

1117. What is the Referral marketing project Management Process?

1118. Did the delivered product meet the specified requirements and goals of the Referral marketing project?

1119. What is the overall risk of the Referral marketing project to your organization?

1120. What were the desired outcomes?

1121. Were the outcomes different from the already stated planned?

1122. How well did the chosen processes fit the needs of the Referral marketing project?

1123. Who are the Referral marketing project stakeholders?

1124. What is an Encumbrance?

1125. Based on your Referral marketing project communication management plan, what worked well?

1126. How well did the chosen processes produce the expected results?

1127. What areas were overlooked on this Referral marketing project?

1128. Is the Referral marketing project funded?

1129. Will the Referral marketing project deliverable(s) replace a current asset or group of assets?

1130. Was the schedule met?

5.1 Procurement Audit: Referral marketing

1131. Are there regular reviews and analysis of the performance of the procurement function/unit?

1132. Do the employees have the necessary skills and experience to carry out procurements efficiently?

1133. Is your organization policy on purchasing covered by a written manual?

1134. Do procedures require cash advances to be returned by transferred or terminated employees before they can receive final paychecks?

1135. Is it assessed whether well-functioning markets exist for the departments services/tasks?

1136. Does the individual having check-signing responsibility review the use of the signature plates?

1137. Was the suitability of candidates accurately assessed?

1138. Does the procurement Referral marketing project comply with European Communities regulations and rules?

1139. Has the department identified and described the different elements in the procurement process?

1140. Do procurement staff, supplier and end user

communicate properly?

1141. Is there no evidence of false certifications?

1142. Are idle funds invested, and is interest distributed to the various activity accounts at least annually?

1143. Is there a purchasing policy as to the amount of an order on which bidding is required?

1144. Are travel expenditures monitored to determine that they are in line with other employees and reasonable for the area of travel?

1145. Are periodic audits made of disbursement activities?

1146. Is it on a regular basis examined whether it is possible to enter into public private partnerships with private suppliers?

1147. Do contracts contain regular reviews, targets and quality standards in order to assess suppliers performance?

1148. Are unusual uses of organization funds investigated?

1149. Are internal control systems in place?

1150. Was the performance description adequate to needs and legal requirements?

5.2 Contract Close-Out: Referral marketing

1151. Change in attitude or behavior?

1152. Has each contract been audited to verify acceptance and delivery?

1153. Was the contract sufficiently clear so as not to result in numerous disputes and misunderstandings?

1154. Are the signers the authorized officials?

1155. Change in knowledge?

1156. Have all acceptance criteria been met prior to final payment to contractors?

1157. Parties: Authorized?

1158. Was the contract type appropriate?

1159. How/when used ?

1160. What happens to the recipient of services?

1161. What is capture management?

1162. Was the contract complete without requiring numerous changes and revisions?

1163. Have all contract records been included in the Referral marketing project archives?

1164. Have all contracts been completed?

1165. Change in circumstances?

1166. How is the contracting office notified of the automatic contract close-out?

1167. Have all contracts been closed?

1168. How does it work?

1169. Parties: who is involved?

5.3 Project or Phase Close-Out: Referral marketing

1170. When and how were information needs best met?

1171. Complete yes or no?

1172. Who exerted influence that has positively affected or negatively impacted the Referral marketing project?

1173. Were risks identified and mitigated?

1174. What was expected from each stakeholder?

1175. In preparing the Lessons Learned report, should it reflect a consensus viewpoint, or should the report reflect the different individual viewpoints?

1176. If you were the Referral marketing project sponsor, how would you determine which Referral marketing project team(s) and/or individuals deserve recognition?

1177. Is the lesson significant, valid, and applicable?

1178. What are the informational communication needs for each stakeholder?

1179. Is the lesson based on actual Referral marketing project experience rather than on independent research?

1180. What is in it for you?

1181. What is a Risk Management Process?

1182. In addition to assessing whether the Referral marketing project was successful, it is equally critical to analyze why it was or was not fully successful. Are you including this?

1183. Did the Referral marketing project management methodology work?

1184. What were the actual outcomes?

1185. Does the lesson describe a function that would be done differently the next time?

1186. What process was planned for managing issues/ risks?

1187. Have business partners been involved extensively, and what data was required for them?

5.4 Lessons Learned: Referral marketing

1188. Were quality procedures built into the Referral marketing project?

1189. How effective were Referral marketing project audits?

1190. How much flexibility is there in the funding (e.g., what authorities does the program manager have to change to the specifics of the funding within the overall funding ceiling)?

1191. Was the user/client satisfied with the end product?

1192. What is the proportion of in-house and contractor personnel authorized for the Referral marketing project?

1193. Who needs to learn lessons?

1194. Whom to share Lessons Learned Information with?

1195. How effective was Referral marketing project Team member training?

1196. How effective was the documentation that you received with the Referral marketing project product/ service?

1197. How well does the product or service the Referral marketing project produced meet the defined Referral marketing project requirements?

1198. What things mattered the most on this Referral marketing project?

1199. How effective was the training you received in preparation for the use of the product/service?

1200. Does the lesson educate others to improve performance?

1201. To what extent was the evolution of risks communicated?

1202. How well did the scope of the Referral marketing project match what was defined in the Referral marketing project Proposal?

1203. How closely did deliverables match what was defined within the Referral marketing project Scope?

1204. What skills did you need that were missing on this Referral marketing project?

1205. Was there a Referral marketing project Definition document. Was there a Referral marketing project Plan. Were they used during the Referral marketing project?

1206. For the next Referral marketing project, how could you improve on the way Referral marketing project was conducted?

Index

Lightning Source UK Ltd.
Milton Keynes UK
UKHW040157060119
334993UK00018B/590/P